MW01670640

Appalachian Social Justice:
Creating a Beloved Community

Appalachian Social Justice
Creating a Beloved Community

ADVANCE REVIEW COPY EDITION

Jessica June Davis, M.Div., J.D., D.Min.

Appalachia Academic Books
www.appalachiabooks.com

Appalachian Social Justice:
Creating a Beloved Community

ISBN 0-9767370-1-9

Published by
Appalachia Academic Books
P.O. Box 33511
Baltimore, Maryland 21218
443-836-0219

Printed in United States of America
Morris Publishing
3212 East Highway 30
Kearney, NE 68847

This Book is Dedicated to the Memory

Mrs. Coretta Scott King
April 27, 1927- January 30, 2006

TABLE OF CONTENTS

Prologue

Good morning. We have gathered here today to remember and celebrate the life of the Reverend Dr. Martin Luther King, Jr. and to keep his dream alive. First, I would like to thank the Carbondale branch of the NAACP and President Carlton Smith for the invitation to speak about one of America's greatest generals for justice. Secondly, I want to take this opportunity to remind each of you to never forget the fifteen-year struggle behind the creation of this national federal holiday.

In 1968, Michigan Congressman John Conyers introduced legislation for a commemorative holiday four days after King's assassination on April 4th on the balcony of the Lorraine Motel in Memphis, Tennessee. The bill stalled in 1968, and in response, six million Americans signed petitions to endorse the holiday. Then, New York Representative Shirley Chisholm joined Congressman Conyers and resubmitted the legislation. They submitted this legislation session after session until 1983. Congress finally passed the holiday legislation and the late President Ronald Reagan signed it into law in 1983. Let us never forget the struggle or we indeed will be destined to repeat it.

As I began to reflect on this general for justice, Dr. Martin Luther King, Jr., in my life's story and the legacy he left for this generation and the generations to follow. I also began to think about another general for justice in my life story. I want to reflect on the Reverend Ida McNeil Davis, and the legacy she left as well. Ida McNeil Davis is my mother. She took her last breath on January 15, 2002 in the same way she took her first breath on July 16, 1930.

As you know January 15th is the birthday of Dr. King. He took his first breath on January 15, 1929. My mother, Reverend Ida Davis, was not only the mother of seven children, but she also represents the mothers of the struggle for justice in America's history who grew up in the segregated south. I can stand before you today because of her "dream being deeply rooted in the American dream," a statement so eloquently articulated by Dr. King.

On July 16, 1930, Linus and Nellie McNeil became the proud parents of Ida McNeil in Lillington, North Carolina. Because her father died prematurely and her mother had to work as a housekeeper to survive, my grandmother, Nellie, sent my mother to live with her father, Marshall McNeil. My great-grandfather was a sharecropper. Yes, I am the great-granddaughter of a sharecropper. Let us never forget the struggle or we indeed will be destined to repeat it.

For those of you who may not know the role of the sharecropper in America's history, let me help you. My great-grandfather did not receive his mule and forty acres of land. Great-grandfather Marshall lived on and harvested the land for a landowner who was a slave owner. Yes, my great-grandfather would never own his land. Sharecropper is another word for indentured servitude or slavery.

My mother grew up in the segregated South. When she graduated from Harnett County High School in Dunn, North Carolina, she was offered a housekeeping job as her graduation gift. This was a great achievement in an environment of many obstacles and at this point in history. Today, in many of our urban and rural communities, young men and women are facing similar or identical obstacles.

An educated housekeeper in the 1940's in the south was an invaluable commodity. My mother breached the visible and invisible social constraints of her time, and said, "No, I am moving north and going to college." She packed her one suitcase and moved to Baltimore, Maryland. She joined the migration of African Americans from the south to the north in pursuit of human dignity, human potential, and social justice.

The pursuits of these two great generals and others in my life's story for human dignity, human potential, and social justice lead me to this moment in time today. I am compelled today by their pursuits and legacies to sound the shofar of justice and speak to America this morning. America will never be the America she so desires to be until she moves from keeping Dr. King's Dream alive to fulfilling the Dream.

So I have come to speak to you, America, about not only keeping the Dream alive of Dr. Martin Luther King, Jr., but to say it is now time to fulfill the Dream. Let us never forget that we are standing on the shoulders of men, women, boys, and girls who suffered and died for the pursuit of the goals of Dr. King's Dream, the pursuit of dignity, human potential, and social justice that is deeply rooted in the "American Dream." We cannot let their deaths ever be in vain. The generations here today listening to the blowing of this shofar of justice have a responsibility.

As I talk to you, America, this morning, I invite you, Mr. Citizen and Mrs. Citizen, to hear me. I invite you, Father Citizen and Mother Citizen, to hear me as well. As I talk to you, America, this morning, I invite you, Son Citizen and Daughter Citizen. I invite you, Sister Citizen and Brother Citizen. I invite you, Aunt Citizen and Uncle Citizen. I also invite you, Illegal Citizen. Yes, you, Illegal Citizen. You know I cannot continue to ignore you because you are here. I recognize that you have put your life in danger to sit in the bosom of America's shores in pursuit of the American Dream. For some, you have put yourselves in danger by the way you arrived and others by the decision to break the immigration laws of this land.

Let me say to you today that your illegal status does not exempt you from taking a role in the destiny of America. You will still be held responsible as the other men and women of this nation are being held responsible today for the destiny of this nation. As an American citizen, we cannot let you continue to drink from the breast of America and not give back to her. We invite you to join us today to help America fulfill her dream. We invite you to sit around the table of injustice until it becomes a table of justice for all. When this happens, America will be the America she is destined to be. Illegal Citizen, if you decide not to join us you will find yourself joining the disenfranchised of this nation and America will never be the America she is so destined to be for you.

There are many categories of citizenship. Today, I want to talk to the American citizen. America, do you hear the sound of the ram's horn calling for a new America to rise out of the ashes of social injustice? I hear my mother's voice today as never before. I hear Dr. King's voice today as well. Both are saying, "The dream must be fulfilled." I am compelled this morning as I have never been compelled before to challenge each of you to fulfill King's dream in your souls, homes, schools, communities, churches, synagogues, mosques, and nation.

Let's stop for a moment. Take this second and look into the eyes of the person sitting on your right. As you look into his or her eyes, you are saying I acknowledge the "dignity, worth, and sacredness of your human personality." Now say to that person, as if your words could move mountains, "I am holding you responsible for the destiny of our nation." Now turn to the person on your left, and say again, "I am holding you responsible for the destiny of our nation." From this point on, look into the eyes of every person you meet until they recognize that you recognize the "dignity, worth, and sacredness of their human personality." Your eyes are the windows to your soul. I can look in your eyes and know whether you hate or love me. We must take responsibility for our own destiny. If we don't, no one else will.

How long will we continue to blame others for what is now our responsibility? The blood of those who suffered and died on the ships, shores, fields, ghettos, and reservations of America cries out from the streets of the nation today for justice. Do you not hear "Rachel weeping for her children" in the streets of New Orleans? We continue to live as if the state of affairs is someone else's problem.

We look for media outlets throughout this nation to give voice to the state of affairs. I would rather that we give our own voices to the state of affairs. For America to be the America that she so desires to be, the state of affairs cannot be relegated to thirty-second sound bites and video clips. This is not necessarily a criticism of the media, rather an understanding of some limitations. Each of us is responsible for giving voice to daily social injustices in our nation.

Are we our brothers' keepers? Yes, we are. If we do nothing, the blood will be on our hands. If we do nothing, a segment of our nation will never know human dignity, human potential, or justice. If we do nothing, the corners of our cities will continue to be an eyesore for the nation as revealed in the mini-series called "The Corner" now running on BET. As revealed during the coal mine tragedies in West Virginia, the hollows of the Appalachian hills of West Virginia will continue to be the aunt in the attic that no one talks about but everyone knows she is there. Each person here today must take responsibility for the destiny of America.

There are those who say we have come a long way. Yes, I would agree. The fact that we are here today, on a national federal holiday, to celebrate the life of one of America's greatest generals for justice validates the progress this nation has made since 1619 when the first slaves arrived in what is now known as the state of Virginia. There are those who also say Affirmative Action programs have run their course and that these programs today are nothing more than acts of reverse discrimination. I cannot say that I agree, but I can say that I understand your position given your reference point. But let me help you understand, with all due respect, what it means to be a well educated and a well traveled great-granddaughter of a sharecropper in America in 2006.

America has not understood the sociological phenomenon of generational memory. It has taken me years of sitting at the feet of my elders, twenty-five plus years of education and reflection, and years of introspective healing to understand why American has not yet fulfilled Dr. King's Dream. Why? We have not understood the phenomenon of generational memory of historically disenfranchised people. The compass of generational memory can be found in the statement: "Let us never forget the struggle or we indeed will be destined to repeat it." This generational memory is a voice of injustice that comes down through the generations until it is heard and finds justice through the life of the one who hears the voice.

As I sat at the feet of world renowned scholars at Harvard Divinity School in the 1990's studying liberation theologies in hope of bringing liberation to the communities I serve, in my mental and emotional state in the classroom, I was actually sitting in the classroom as my mother in the 1930's sitting on the floor in front of a fireplace burning her legs (therefore my legs) until she had permanent white spots shown to me by her when I was a child trying to study and stay warm. This is the fireplace of the home on the land that would never be owned by my great-grandfather but taken by the children's children of the slave owner. This is the duality of the soul created by the generational memory.

The disenfranchised live in both the present and past simultaneously until the voice of the past is heard and addressed. This reflection leads me to another example of my daily duality and struggle. As I sat on a plane on my way to Africa for the first time to talk to thousands of women about entrepreneurship, in my mental and emotional state on the plane at that moment, I was actually sitting on the plane as the woman of yesterday sitting at the bottom of a slave ship after being kidnapped from my motherland to be treated as cattle returning home to say I survived. This voice of injustice also brings the wounds of injustice. The wound of injustice in its generational silence brings anger and rage.

Many never give voices to the injustices because the wounds are so deep and long. The choice becomes either paralysis or rage in daily life in the presence of these memories. The historically disenfranchised here today understand the silent pain of the generations searching for a voice in this generation and the paralysis that can come. Many of our children are not choosing paralysis but rage.

I have come to realize something over the last twenty years. There is a third choice not taken by many. The third choice is healing. We can no longer wait for America to apologize for atrocities they committed against so many. The disenfranchised of this nation must take their power back from the ones who have historically taken the power and allow the healing to take place so we can pursue human dignity, human potential, and justice and fulfill Dr. King's Dream.

First, we must give voice to the pain by identifying the sources. Then we must forgive America. We then must allow ourselves to mourn the great loss of family, life, liberty, and land. If we do nothing, the next generation is in grave danger.

Our children's children are calling from the wombs of eternity for us to take responsibility for the destiny of America. We are the ones that determine our destinies.

To my American brothers and sisters who don't understand what it means to be historically disenfranchised in America, I am not asking you to feel sorry for me. I am not asking you to put another dollar into programs that clearly are not working as they are designed. The only thing that I am asking of you today is that you sit at the table of injustice with me and look me in my eyes until it becomes a table of justice for all.

Dr. King is speaking today to us through his pursuits and legacy of justice. I believe he is saying, "We must hold each other responsible for the destiny of America, because she is waiting for the Dream to be fulfilled." In 1958, Dr. King said in his book, *Stride Toward Freedom,* that all life is interrelated. He also said, "All humanity is involved in a single process, and all men are brothers. To the degree that I harm my brother, no matter what he is doing to me, to that extent I am harming myself." He adds by saying, "If you harm me, you harm yourself."

My brothers and sisters, the Dream must be fulfilled. Because of the interrelatedness of humanity as so eloquently described by Dr. King, if one of our children suffers, all of our children suffer. For America to be the America that she so desires to be, all of America must take responsibility and sit at the table of injustice until it becomes the table of justice for all.

As I close this morning, I want to invite each of you to join me in creating a beloved community by logging onto *http://www.belovednation.com.* This virtual community exists without the constraints of daily life such as location and personal schedules. You can log on from anywhere in the nation at any time and become a virtual citizen of a community pursuing justice for all. This virtual community represents one of my efforts in fulfilling the Rev. Dr. Martin Luther King, Jr.'s Dream. This initiative will be launched nationally next Monday, January 23, 2006. Register today.

American citizen, let's keep the Dream alive by fulfilling the Dream until "justice rolls down like waters and righteousness like a mighty stream." God bless America.

Submitted by
Dr. Jessica June Davis
"Keep the Dream Alive" Speech
Martin Luther King Breakfast
NAACP Carbondale Branch
Carbondale, Illinois
January 16, 2006

Introduction

In America, historically disenfranchised communities, people of color and women, have a heritage of isolation and voicelessness as a result of the human condition: the sins of classism, racism and sexism. The passion for this action research project has grown out of this heritage into a civic responsibility of empowering historically disadvantaged people to the extent that they are able to come out of economic, emotional, social, and spiritual isolation, and voicelessness.

This civic responsibility has given birth to this action research project, the "Appalachian Study Circle for Social Justice: Creating a Beloved Community." The context utilized in this research project is an Appalachian community, Morgantown, in West Virginia. The context of this research project provided an unprecedented opportunity for the researcher, as a community leader, to utilize her passion for community empowerment to develop and implement a twenty-first century model for addressing social injustice in Appalachian communities.

The implemented project, the Beloved Community Study Circle, sponsored by Greater Saint Paul African

Methodist Episcopal Church, asked the community of Morgantown, West Virginia to face a critical issue-how to build a Beloved Community. The Study Circle asked the community of Morgantown to get involved in an online community discussion by examining Dr. Martin Luther King, Jr.'s teachings on the Beloved Community and the nonviolent resistance method as tools to address issues of social injustices in the community. There was an opportunity for people from all backgrounds and all parts of the community to participate in this constructive online conversation, and to propose ways to build a Beloved Community as an individual change agent. [1]

The Beloved Community Study Circle progressed over four consecutive weeks starting with a session on personal experience ("How does social injustice affect me?") to sessions providing broader perspectives ("What are others saying about social injustice?") to a session on action ("What can I do about the social injustice in my community?"). The goal of the Study Circle was to address the issues of economic, emotional, social and spiritual isolation and voicelessness of people of color and women in Morgantown, West Virginia.

The participants, known as the citizens, of the Beloved Community Study Circle stated that the "Appalachian Study Circle for Social Justice: Creating a Beloved Community" was

---

[1]Catherine Flavin-McDonald and Martha L. McCoy, *Facing the Challenges of Racism and Race Relations* (Promfret: Topfields Foundation, Inc., 1997), 36.

a good program and should continue with the development of other online communities. The citizens' knowledge of the new guided study circle methodology developed for this action research project increased as a result of their participation. The citizens' understanding of the nonviolence resistance method increased as a result of completing the module on Nonviolent Resistance. The citizens' comprehension of the Beloved Community methodology also increased as a result of the module on the Beloved Community.

The citizens' knowledge of the landmark Civil Rights cases also increased as a result of the module on the landmark Civil Rights cases. The citizens stated that their understanding of their attitudes and beliefs increased after completing the four modules, and their understanding of others' attitudes and beliefs also increased as a result of participating in the Study Circle. The citizens gave the "Appalachian Study Circle for Social Justice: Creating a Beloved Community" an overall rating of good to very good.

In conclusion, the participants of the Study Circle educated themselves on the issue of social justice, established new relationships, recognized ways to change their own behaviors, and learned how to become a change agent in their community.[2] The next five chapters will provide a detailed

---

[2]Ibid.

narrative analysis of the development and implementation of this action research project, the "Appalachian Study Circle for Social Justice: Creating a Beloved Community." The next chapter reveals the birthing of the passion for this project.

Chapter One

THE STATE OF THE ART IN THE PROJECT

Introduction: The Synergetic Analysis

This section, a synergetic analysis of the action research project, pairs the researcher's background with the needs of the context being observed in the research project. This pairing creates a point of intersection between the researcher's background and context of the research. This point of intersection is called "synergy." The context of this research project, Morgantown,West Virginia, provides an unprecedented opportunity for the researcher as a community leader to utilize her passion for community empowerment. It also allows her to develop and implement a twenty-first century model for addressing social injustice in Appalachian communities. The point of intersection for this project came out of the researcher's experience as an African American woman and community leader living and working in West Virginia as Assistant Dean of Multicultural Affairs and Retention Services at Wheeling Jesuit University. The passion born from this intersection is the "Appalachian Study Circles for Social Justice: Creating a Beloved Community."

Appalachian Study Circle for Social Justice

The research project began at the Young Women's Christian Association of Wheeling (YWCA) in Wheeling, West Virginia with a focus on racism and race relations and ended at Greater Saint Paul African Methodist Episcopal (AME) Church in Morgantown, West Virginia with a focus on social justice. The concept of the action research project developed out of the researcher's position as the Diversity and Leadership Development Consultant for the Young Women's Christian Association of Wheeling. In this role, the YWCA asked her to develop and coordinate a study circle. The program was to be developed according to the model provided by the Study Circles Resource Center (SCRC) with a focus on racism and race relations. During the initial implementation of this SCRC study circle in Wheeling, the researcher noted that Appalachian communities have a legacy of isolation and voicelessness. She quickly realized that she needed to change the strategy for implementing a successful study circle in an Appalachian community. This realization led to the development of the curriculum for her action research project, the Beloved Community Study Circle.

The first challenge with the SCRC study circle was the difficulty of attracting diverse groups of Appalachians. It was very hard to bring diverse groups of Appalachians, with different perspectives, to the table to discuss the issues of racism and race relations in their community. Based on the feedback from her professional peers in the West Virginia, she expanded the focus from race relations to social justice in order to increase the diversity of people and perspectives in the discussions. The discussions incorporated not just racism but also social injustices including sexism and classism.

The researcher was able to expand the focus of the study circle with this new curriculum and methodology in order to encourage more types of people to get involved in discussing and addressing community issues. Some participants felt more comfortable talking about social injustice issues in general rather than focusing just on racism and race relations. The expanded focus required the development of a new curriculum and methodology. This new curriculum and methodology was named the Appalachian Study Circle for Social Justice. The other challenge addressed in the initial development and implementation of this new type of study circle was the issue of scheduling meeting times that fit each participant's schedule. This challenge served as the impetus to creating an online study circle community. The online community allowed participants to participate according to their personal schedules and availability. The final implementation of the project took place in Morgantown, West Virginia with Greater Saint Paul AME Church serving as the sponsoring faith-based organization.

The Beloved Community Study Circle, a project sponsored by Greater Saint Paul AME Church, asked the community of Morgantown, West Virginia to face a critical issue—how to build a Beloved Community. The Study Circle asked the community of Morgantown to get involved in an online community discussion by examining Dr. Martin Luther King, Jr.'s teachings on the Beloved Community and nonviolence resistance method as tools to address issues of social injustices in our community. There was an opportunity for people from all backgrounds and all parts of the community to participate in this constructive online conversation, and propose ways to build a Beloved Community as an individual change agent.[3]

The study circle progressed over four consecutive weeks starting with a session on personal experience ("How does social injustice affect me?") to sessions providing broader perspectives ("What are others saying about social injustice?") to a session on action ("What can I do about the social injustice in my community?"). The participants of the Study Circle educated themselves on the issue of social justice, established new relationships, recognized ways to change their own

---

[3] Catherine Flavin-McDonald and Martha L. McCoy, *Facing the Challenges of Racism and Race Relations* (Promfret: Topfields Foundation, Inc., 1997), 36.

behaviors, and learned how to become a change agent in their community.[4]

The goal of the study circle is to address the issues of economic, emotional, social and spiritual isolation and voicelessness of people of color and women in Morgantown, West Virginia. This research project is the point of intersection between the context and the researcher's background. The next section will describe the source for the development of this new study circle methodology.

Study Circles: The Paul J. Aicher Foundation

In 1982, a nonprofit, nonpartisan foundation, The Paul J. Aicher Foundation, formerly called the Topsfield Foundation, Inc., began with the mission to build community and improve the quality of public life. The Foundation empowers people to participate in public life, to address community concerns, and to take active roles in community decision-making through study circles.[5]

In 1989, the Foundation established the Study Circles Resource Center (SCRC) to promote public deliberation on

---

[4]Ibid.

[5] The Paul J. Aicher Foundation. "Study Circle Resource Center," http://www.studycircles.org/en/ Page.AicherFoundation.aspx (accessed July 10, 2005).

important social and political issues. SCRC began to look for models of people coming together for democratic discussions. They discovered a model developed in New York during the 1870's called the Chautauqua Literary and Scientific Circle. In this study circle, the participants learned from each other in an interactive, collaborative manner. In addition to this nineteenth century model, SCRC studied the work of the National Issues Forums, Industrial Areas Foundation and others. Their research culminated in the launch of a community-wide study circle program on race relations in Lima, Ohio. SCRC developed a model for community-wide dialogue from the Lima program and other community-wide study circle programs. SCRC has served as the source for the initial development of the Appalachian Study Circle for Social Justice.

The contribution of this project to the study circle methodology is the development of a guided educational social justice curriculum. This curriculum is based on Dr. Martin Luther King, Jr.'s teachings on the Beloved Community and nonviolent resistance methods designed for a diverse twenty-first century online Appalachian community. The next section will describe the history of Appalachia and the legacy of economic, emotional, social and spiritual isolation and voicelessness.[6]

---

[6]Ibid.

Appalachia: The First and Last Frontier

The context being utilized in the research project is an Appalachian community, Morgantown, in West Virginia. Why did the researcher choose an Appalachian community as her context? She chose Appalachia for the context of her research project because of the heritage of economic, emotional, social and spiritual isolation, and voicelessness. The next section will describe the history of Appalachia and the legacy of isolation and voicelessness.

The Appalachians: America's First and Last Frontier describes Appalachia as a unique American place deeply rooted in American popular culture. According to *The Appalachians*, when people think of Appalachia, they think of *The Waltons*, one of the most beloved American television dramas of the twenty-first century. In popular culture, the people of Appalachia are portrayed as the "poor souls who live in the hills and hollers." These stereotypical images have contributed to the isolation and voicelessness of the people of Appalachia.[7]

Appalachia actually incorporates two hundred thousand square miles of more than twenty-three million people. These twenty-three million people claim the Appalachian

[7] Mari-Lynn Evans and others, eds. *The Appalachians: America's First and Last Frontier* (New York: Random House, 2004), xx.

geographical and cultural identity. The Appalachian region includes West Virginia and parts of Alabama, Georgia, Kentucky, Maryland, Mississippi, New York, North Carolina, Ohio, Pennsylvania, South Carolina, Tennessee, and Virginia. The spine of Appalachia is the Appalachian mountain range that runs down the eastern part of the United States including the Green Mountains of Vermont, White Mountains of New Hampshire, Allegheny Mountains, Blue Ridge Mountains, and Great Smoky Mountains.[8]

According to *The Appalachians,* Appalachia was America's first frontier. The original inhabitants of Appalachia were the Iroquois, Chickasaw, Choctaw, and Cherokee Indians. In the early 1700's, English, German, Scottish, and Irish settlers joined these indigenous people. These Protestant settlers established Presbyterian, Methodist, Lutheran, Baptist, and Pentecostal rural churches in Appalachia as an expression of their Christian heritage. As a result of these Appalachian settlers, the region's religious practices, social customs, traditions and music were greatly influenced by the British Isles.[9]

The legacy of isolation and voicelessness can be traced in part to the geographical isolation created by the

---

[8] Ibid., xxi.

[9] Ibid.

Appalachian's mountainous terrain. The mountainous terrain created isolated communities in the eighteenth and nineteenth centuries. The vast Appalachian mountain range hindered westward expansion. As a result of the mountainous terrain, many communities still remain isolated from each other and the rest of the nation today. This geographical isolation has manifested itself in all aspects of life in Appalachia.[10]

Blacks had a unique situation in the history of Appalachia. There were slaves in almost every county of Appalachia. However, most families owned less than five slaves because most of the region did not have large plantations and the families could not afford slaves. According to *The Appalachians,* approximately ten percent of the region was Black prior to the Civil War. During Reconstruction, in the late nineteenth and early twentieth centuries, Blacks migrated to Appalachian communities for the growing coal mining opportunities. [11]

The growing demand for coal as America became an international industrial power necessitated the development of the Appalachian railroad system in West Virginia and central Appalachia and the creation of coal company owned and operated towns. The families of the miners lived in these

---

[10]Ibid.

[11]Ibid., xxiii.

towns, and the children went to coal company owned and operated schools. The miners were paid with scrip instead of United States currency. The coal company currency required the miners and their families to buy their goods only at the coal company store. [12]

Senator Robert Byrd of West Virginia remembered living by a mining town, Sotesbury, owned by a typical coal company. He remembered the miners working all day from dawn to dusk for two dollars a day paid in scrip in the early 1900's. Senator Byrd also recalled when unions came to the mines, and when it became lawful for miners to engage in collective bargaining for better wages and working conditions. Unionization created a spirit of hope for the people of Appalachia according to Senator Bryd. However, this spirit would not be fully realized by all because the industry became highly mechanized. As a result, this technological shift forced many miners to leave West Virginia in search of work. In 1952, when Senator Bryd ran for Congress, he recalled that there were more than 125,000 coal miners and there are only 20,000 today. This shift in the industry severely impacted the financial infrastructure of the region.[13]

---

[12] Ibid., xxiv.

[13] Ibid., 123.

Congressman Alan B. Mollohan's commentary on the history of West Virginia in *The Appalachians* reiterates Senator Bryd's historical assessment of the coal industry in West Virginia. The first mistake described by Congressman Mollohan is the historical outside ownership of West Virginia resources. According to Congressman Mollohan, the outside ownership of West Virginia resources became a rule rather than an exception. As a result of these significant outside interests, few profits were reinvested to diversify the economy.[14]

The entire infrastructure of West Virginia grew around a narrow industrial sector owned by outsiders. As a result, the infrastructure of West Virginia became vulnerable to industry changes. Congressman Mollohan believes West Virginia paid a heavy price for this lack of strategic planning in the form of lost resources, profits, opportunities, and people.[15]

This significant economic change in West Virginia and other Appalachian communities moved the people from a place of pride and independence to a place of complete dependency on outsiders, outsiders who exploited the natural resources and people of Appalachia according to *The Appalachians*. In the early 1900's, labor wars flared between miners and management as miners began to demand better wages and working conditions. In the 1960's, the federal government

[14] Ibid., 153.

[15] Ibid.

created the Appalachian Regional Commission to begin to address some of the injustices of the region. However, this economic exploitation had already made a significant contribution to the legacy of isolation and voicelessness experienced by the people of Appalachia. The next section will describe the current demographical context of the research project.[16]

United States Bureau of the Census

The United States is becoming an increasingly diverse society according to the United States Bureau of the Census. Immigration has played a major role in the increasing the diversity of the U.S. according to the "YWCA Racial Justice Training Manual." The foreign-born population makes up more than 10 % of the U.S. population. In 2000, the U.S. Bureau of the Census estimated the United States population to be 281,400,000-75.1%White, 12.3% Black, 12.5% Hispanic, 3.6 % Asian & Pacific Islander, and 0.9% Native American. By 2050, according to the projections of the U.S. Bureau, Asian, non-Hispanic Black, Hispanic, and American Indian populations will be close to 50% of the U.S. population.

---

[16] Ibid., xxiv.

West Virginia Context

The diversity in West Virginia is significantly less than the national demographics, but it reveals the increased challenge of addressing social injustice in West Virginia of men and women experiencing isolation and voicelessness. However, the smaller population of Morgantown makes it more practical to create a model for addressing social injustice for other Appalachian communities.

The population of West Virginia is 1,766,196- 95.1% White, 3.1% Black, 0.7% Hispanic, 0.5% Asian & Pacific Islander, and 0.1 % Native American according to the United States Bureau of the Census. The initial context for this project was Wheeling, West Virginia. The population of Wheeling, West Virginia is 31,419, 92.7% White, 5.0% Black, 0.6% Hispanic, 0.9% Asian & Pacific Islander, and 0.1% Native American according to the United States Bureau of the Census.

The final context for the research project is Morgantown, West Virginia. The population of Morgantown, West Virginia and the context of the Appalachian Study Circle for Social Justice is 26, 809, 89.5%White, 4.2%Black, 1.5%Hispanic, 4.2%Asian & Pacific Islander, and 0.2% Native American. The next section will describe the initial context for the development of the Appalachian Study Circle with the focus on racism and race relations. This initial context is crucial because the YWCA Wheeling served as the impetus for the development of this action research project, and the next section gives additional historical insight about the region and nation in the context of racial and gender injustice.

National YWCA Context

What is the legacy of the YWCA that provided the initial context for the development of this action research project? The YWCA began as a movement in England in 1855 according to the YWCA of Wheeling. Then in 1858, the movement came to the United States. A small group of Protestant women of various denominations began to work together for the empowerment of women. These women had a religious based concern for the worth of all human beings. During the conception and expansion of the YWCA, religious revival was sweeping through the northeast.[17]

In 1859, Boston opened the first branch of the YWCA. New York followed with the opening of a new branch in 1860 that included a boarding house for young women. Then in 1867 branches opened in Hartford, Pittsburgh, Cleveland, and Cincinnati. The first student branch of the YWCA began in 1873 at Illinois State University. By 1875, there were twenty-

---

[17] Carmen Rivera-Watson, ed., "Racial Justice Training Manual," (New York: YWCA of the U.S.A., 1996), 18.

eight YWCAs. "The Young Women's Christian Association pioneered in the task of working against racial discrimination toward full integration, fighting obvious segregation practices and exposing hidden patterns of discrimination in legislation, institutions, and systems." The story of the YWCA of the U.S. is a chapter in the history of the civil rights movement according to the "YWCA Racial Justice Training Manual."[18]

Wheeling YWCA Context

In 1905, Miss Helen M. Coale, student secretary of Virginia and West Virginia for the American Committee of the YWCA, came to Wheeling to establish a local YWCA. She met with a number of women at the First Presbyterian Church to discuss the viability of a local association. The women decided to call a meeting of Protestant Evangelical Churches. On December 9, 1905, these women held the meeting at the Young Men's Christian Association, and approved the establishment of a local YWCA. On April 9, 1906, the YWCA of Wheeling became a permanent organization. During this April meeting, a constitution was adopted and thirty women were elected to the Board of Directors.[19]

---

[18]Ibid.

In 1921, Mrs. Sarah Robinson, an employee at the Central YWCA in Wheeling, West Virginia, contacted, Mrs. Mindel, the House Mother, to discuss the establishment of a "Negro" branch of the YWCA in Wheeling. Mrs. Mary Bank, wife of a prominent "Negro" physician, felt the same need for a "Negro" branch in Wheeling. As a result of this realized need, a survey was created and distributed to determine the viability of this new branch. As a result of the survey, Mrs. Codelle Winn, an African American secretary from the National Board, came to the Central Association and approved a new Wheeling branch.

Twelve African American women were chosen to serve on the Management Committee of the new Branch. Miss Mary L. McMechen served as the first Chair. Miss Escobeda Serreals, a Girl Reserve worker, became the first Executive Director two months later. After Miss Serreals' appointment, the Branch held a contest to select an appropriate name and symbol for the Branch. The judges chose "The Blue Triangle Branch of the Young Women's Christian Association." The Branch officially opened their doors on June 21, 1921. Then in

---

[19]Mary R. Gordon, "Historical Sketch of the Y.W.C.A." (Wheeling, West Virginia: Y.W.C.A.. 1916), typewritten.

June of 1956, the Central YWCA and the Blue Triangle YWCA decided to combine and become completely integrated.[20]

The One Imperative

In 1970, 2,709 YWCA delegates from over 372 communities, came together and adopted a formal resolution called the "Imperative," at the National YWCA Convention held in Houston, Texas according to the "YWCA Racial Justice Training Manual." The resolution, goal statement, expressed these words: "To thrust our collective power toward the elimination of racism wherever it exists and by any means necessary." This resolution grew out of the concerns of racial justice in the U.S. and the role of the YWCA articulated during the eight "Racial Justice Institutes" held by the YWCA in 1969. In 1985, this resolution became part of the YWCA's Constitution. This is the legacy of race relations for the YWCA Appalachian Study Circles in Wheeling, West Virginia and this legacy led to the initial development of the Appalachian Study Circle in Wheeling, West Virginia.[21]

---

[20]Mary R. Gordon, "Historical Sketch of the Y.W.C.A." (Wheeling, West Virginia: Y.W.C.A. 1916), typewritten.

[21]Carmen Rivera-Watson, ed., "Racial Justice Training Manual," (New York: YWCA of the U.S.A., 1996), 17.

The next section will discuss the final context for the implementation of the Appalachian Study Circle for Social Justice. Given the expanded focus of the Appalachian Study Circle for Social Justice, the mission of the African Methodist Episcopal Church, and interest of the senior pastor, Greater St. Paul AME Church became an appropriate context for the implementation of the final version of this action research project.

Greater Saint Paul African Methodist Episcopal Church

The Greater Saint Paul AME Church of Morgantown, West Virginia was established in 1871 on land deeded through the estate of John Hoffman, Sr. according to the pastor, Reverend Angela V. Walker. The church constructed a one-room structure facing the Monongalia River at a later date. According to *The Doctrine and Discipline of the African Methodist Episcopal Church*, the mission and purpose of Greater Saint Paul AME Church is to minister to the spiritual, intellectual, physical, emotional, and environmental needs of all people through word and deed of the original Free African Society, out of which the African Methodist Episcopal Church developed.[22]

In November of 1787, the founding members of the African Methodist Episcopal Church gathered to discuss the growing mistreatment by white members of the Methodist Society in Philadelphia. Mistreatment such as being pulled off their knees while praying and sent back to their seats. In 1793, Richard Allen proposed the building of the African Methodist meeting house on his own land at his own expense.[23] The African Methodist Episcopal Church was created in the late eighteenth century.

The African Methodist Episcopal Church and Greater Saint Paul African Methodist Episcopal Church have fought the enemies of justice, freedom and brotherhood for over two hundred years according to *The Doctrine and Discipline.* [24] The AME Church is committed to a ministry of liberation.[25] As the Church fulfills this mission of justice, the Greater Saint Paul AME Church is also committed to identifying itself with the value system, which has grown out of the Black Appalachian experience with God.[26] The legacy of the African Methodist

---

[22]John Hurst Adams and others, eds. *The Doctrine and Discipline of the African Methodist Episcopal Church* (Tennessee: The AMEC Sunday School Union, 1997), 12.

[23]Ibid., 5.

[24] Ibid.,1.

[25] Ibid.,2.

[26]Ibid., 3.

Episcopal Church and Greater Saint Paul AME Church made Greater Saint Paul the ideal partner and sponsor for the final implementation of the Appalachian Study Circle for Social Justice. The next section will provide the conclusion to this chapter.

Conclusion

The Appalachian context of this project provides an unprecedented opportunity for the researcher as a community leader to utilize her passion for community empowerment, to develop and implement a model for addressing issues of social injustice in Morgantown, West Virginia and other Appalachian communities.

The goal of the Appalachia Study Circle for Social Justice is to address the issues of economic, emotional, social and spiritual isolation and voicelessness of Appalachian people of Morgantown, West Virginia. This research project is the point of intersection between this Appalachian context and the researcher's community empowerment background. The next chapter will provide the theoretical foundation for the development of the Appalachian Study Circle for Social Justice, the Beloved Community Study Circle.

Chapter Two

APPALACHIAN THEORETICAL FOUNDATION

The Making of Appalachian Liberation Theology

Introduction

The Appalachian Study Circle for Social Justice: Creating a Beloved Community, a project sponsored by the Greater Saint Paul AME Church, calls for the development of a liberation theology. This call brings the researcher to the following question: "What is the theological foundation of the Appalachian Study Circle for Social Justice being held in West Virginia?" The theological foundation requires a new Appalachian contextualized theological system of liberation with the goal of eradicating social injustice in West Virginia and other Appalachian communities. The legacy of this new liberation theology can be traced backed to the 1960's and the development of Black theology. This chapter explores the need for the development of a new Appalachian system of theological reflection by discussing the legacy of Black theology. This new theological system will be called "Appalachian Liberation Theology." However, before the researcher could explore the development of this new twenty-first century liberation theology, she had to understand the historical, philosophical, and theological schools of thought of the twentieth century.

Judeo-Christian Theology

According to "Black Theology in the Making" by J. Deotis Roberts, theology is a discipline of interpretation of revelation, the process of divine unveiling.[27] Theology is reflection upon the experience of revelation.[28] The experience of revelation cannot be separated from the social context. According to "Biblical Revelation and Social Existence," theology is shaped by socially determined values.[29] Therefore, a theological system is not complete without an investigation of the system's social context.[30]

---

[27] James H. Cone and Wilmore, Gayraud S., *Black Theology: A Documentary History, Volume I: 1966-1979. (*Maryknoll, New York. Orbis Books, 1993), 114.

[28] Ibid, 115.

[29] James H. Cone and Wilmore, Gayraud S., *Black Theology: A Documentary History, Volume I: 1966-1979. (*Maryknoll, New York. Orbis Books, 1993), 159.

[30] Ibid.

According to "Black Theology and Black Liberation," Black theology is a phenomenon of the 1960's, relatively new to America.[31] Black theology developed out of the need of African Americans to think theologically about their oppression.[32] The birth of Black theology represents the first attempt by African American ministers and scholars to define the faith of Black American Protestantism in the context of the history of oppression and slavery.[33] Black theology can be described as the religious counterpart of the secular movement of the 1960's called "Black Power."[34] The "Black Power" movement appeared in the spring of 1966.[35] According to James Cone, the author of "A Black Theology of Liberation," "Black Power" is recognition that Black freedom is dependent on Blacks doing whatever is necessary to end the victimization of White racism and reclaim human dignity.[36]

---

[31] Ibid., 106.

[32] Ibid., 15.

[33] Ibid., 89.

[34] Ibid., 106.

[35] Ibid., 108.

[36] Ibid., 109.

According to the "Statement by the National Committee of Black Churchmen" in June of 1969, Black theology places the Black condition of oppression in the light of Judeo-Christian tradition.[37] "The message of liberation is the revelation of God as revealed in the incarnation of Jesus Christ."[38] Black theology also places the Black condition in the Old Testament by identifying with Israel's liberation. Israel's liberation in the Old Testament comes solely from the power of Yahweh.[39] God's will is identical with the liberation of the oppressed from social and political bondage.[40] Therefore, Judeo-Christian theology requires political involvement that makes a stand against disenfranchisement, isolation and voicelessness.[41]

The God of Judeo-Christian theology is involved in human history and this is unlike the God of Greek philosophy that is removed from history.[42] The Old Testament is the drama

---

[37] James H. Cone and Wilmore, Gayraud S., *Black Theology: A Documentary History, Volume I: 1966-1979. (*Maryknoll, New York. Orbis Books, 1993), 38.

[38] Ibid.

[39] Ibid.,162.

[40] Ibid.

[41] Ibid.

[42] Ibid., 160.

of God's mighty acts in history.[43] "In the Exodus-Sinai tradition Yahweh is disclosed as the God of history, whose revelation is identical with his power to liberate the oppressed."[44]

Black theology as a Judeo-Christian theology is a discipline that analyzes the meaning of God's liberation in light of Jesus Christ.[45] "Taking seriously the necessity to make the Christian message of liberation relevant to our time, we conclude that Christian theology in America must also be Black."[46] In other words, Judeo-Christian theological reflection must come out of the Black experience. This theological legacy led to the making of a new theological system called the Appalachian liberation theology.

Liberation Theology

According to "Black Theology and Third World Theologies" by James H. Cone, liberation theology is created in the struggles of the disenfranchised. We cannot participate in the liberation of the disenfranchised from oppression unless we know who the disenfranchised are and why they live in this

---

[43] Ibid.

[44] Ibid., 161.

[45] Ibid., 109.

[46] Ibid., 112.

state of disenfranchisement. Therefore, liberation theology requires social analysis, a tool that helps us to know why certain social, economic, and political orders exist. Social analysis is also the legacy of this new theological reflection, Appalachian liberation theology.[47]

Appalachian Liberation Theology

What is the theological foundation of the Appalachian Study Circle on Social Justice being held in Appalachian communities in West Virginia? The theological foundation of the Appalachian Study Circle on Social Justice is the making of Appalachian liberation theology.

What is Appalachian liberation theology? Appalachian liberation theology is a discipline of the interpretation of experiences of revelation in Appalachia concerning social injustices.[48] Appalachian liberation theology is a Judeo-Christian theology. Appalachian liberation theology places the Appalachian condition of isolation and voicelessness in the

---

[47] James H. Cone and Wilmore, Gayraud S., *Black Theology: A Documentary History, Volume II: 1980-1992. (*Maryknoll, New York. Orbis Books, 1993), 393.

[48] James H. Cone and Wilmore, Gayraud S., *Black Theology: A Documentary History, Volume I: 1966-1979. (*Maryknoll, New York. Orbis Books, 1993), 115.

light of the Judeo-Christian tradition.[49] Judeo-Christian theology in West Virginia must be Appalachian.[50] In other words, Judeo-Christian theological reflection must include the experiences of the people of Appalachia.

Appalachian liberation theology is being created in the struggles of the disenfranchised of the Appalachian communities of West Virginia. According to James Cone, we cannot participate in the liberation of the disenfranchised unless we know who the disenfranchised are and why they are in a state of disenfranchisement. Therefore, Appalachian liberation theology requires social analysis because theology is shaped by socially determined values.[51] The tool of social analysis for the Appalachian liberation theology is the Appalachian Study Circle for Social Justice. This action research project serves as one of the first efforts to develop a tool that allows the practitioners of theology to know why certain social, economic, and political orders exist and how we can begin to respond.[52]

In conclusion, God is involved in the history of social justice in Appalachia. According to Appalachian theological

---

[49] Ibid., 38.

[50] Ibid., 112.

[51] Ibid., 159.

[52] James H. Cone and Wilmore, Gayraud S., *Black Theology: A Documentary History, Volume II: 1980-1992. (*Maryknoll, New York. Orbis Books, 1993), 393.

reflection, the message of liberation articulated by the study circle methodology is a tool that is revealing the God of history.[53] God is involved in the eradication of social injustice in Appalachia in order that the disenfranchised can reclaim their human dignity and create the Beloved Community.

Appalachian liberation theology is a new phenomenon of the twenty-first century.[54] Appalachian liberation theology is developing out of the need of Appalachian communities to think theologically about their isolation and voicelessness and how to respond to the legacy of social injustice.[55] The creation of the Appalachian liberation theology represents the first self-conscious attempt by an Appalachian community leader and researcher to define the faith of Appalachian Americans in the context of a history of isolation and voicelessness.[56] This is the making of Appalachian liberation theology. The next section will describe the methodology of the Appalachian Study Circle for Social Justice.

---

[53] James H. Cone and Wilmore, Gayraud S., *Black Theology: A Documentary History, Volume I: 1966-1979.* (Maryknoll, New York. Orbis Books, 1993), 38.

[54] Ibid., 106.

[55] Ibid., 15.

[56] James H. Cone and Wilmore, Gayraud S., *Black Theology: A Documentary History, Volume I: 1966-1979.* (Maryknoll, New York. Orbis Books, 1993), 89.

Chapter Three

THE METHODOLOGY

Beloved Community Study Circle: Creating a Beloved Community in West Virginia

Introduction

The Beloved Community Study Circle, an online program sponsored by Greater Saint Paul African Methodist Episcopal Church, asked the community of Morgantown, West Virginia to face a critical issue—how to build a Beloved Community. The Study Circle asked the community of Morgantown to get involved in an online community discussion by examining Dr. Martin Luther King, Jr.'s teachings on the Beloved Community as a tool to address issues of social injustices in their community. There was an opportunity for people from all backgrounds and all parts of the community to participate in this constructive online conversation, and propose ways to build a Beloved Community as an individual change agent.

The Study Circle coordinator looked for people interested in addressing social injustice in their community to participate in this four-week cutting-edge online pilot program.

The participants were asked to read and respond to weekly discussion questions on the "Question & Answer" page of the website,*http://www.belovednation.com,* at their own convenience. The weekly discussion questions were posted on the website on the Mondays of each week by noon. After responding to the weekly questions, the participants were invited to participate in the online discussion board with other study circle participants by sharing their reflections on creating the Beloved Community. The Study Circle coordinator provided a question or statement on the "Join Discussion" page to start the weekly discussions. The participants were invited to participate in the discussions daily. Finally, the participants were invited to provide weekly journal entries of their thoughts on creating a Beloved Community on the "Journal" page. The Study Circle coordinator informed the participants that at the end of the program, the results of the Study Circle would be documented, posted online, and published. The coordinator also informed the participants that their names would be kept confidential.

The Appalachian Study Circle began Monday, April 4, 2005 and continued for four weeks. Each selected participant received compensation for their participation after they submitted their exit surveys. The next section discusses the first module of the Beloved Community Study Circle.

Beloved Community Study Circle Module One

The first week of the online community began with the presentation and question, "What is the Beloved Community Study Circle?" The Beloved Community Study Circle is an online community of people from diverse backgrounds. The members of this community discuss and acquire skills to address critical social justice issues in their community over a period of four weeks. Four consecutive online modules guide the discussions: one module on personal experiences, two modules examining other perspectives including landmark Civil Rights cases, and a module on becoming an individual change agent in their community.[57]

The module then moved to the presentation and question, "What is the ultimate tragedy of slavery and segregation in America?" The system of slavery and segregation made African Americans feel inferior. This system of oppression scarred the soul and distorted the personality of African Americans. This system gave the oppressor privileges and a false sense of superiority.[58]

---

[57] Sarah Campbell, Amy Malick, and Martha McCoy. *Organizing Community-wide Dialogue for Action and Change.* Topsfield Foundation, Inc.: 2001

[58] Martin Luther King Jr." The Current Crisis in Race Relations." *New South (March 1958): 8-12.*

Then after presenting the questions and responses at the beginning of the module, the module then presented the question, "Do you agree with this statement on the tragedy of slavery and segregation? Why or Why not?" Each participant answered in writing and discussed the subject online with other participants, the citizens of the community.

The next segment of the online community began with the presentation and question, "How will the struggle against injustice be waged?" There are two answers to this question. The first answer is violence. Violence never solves social problems. Violence actually creates new problems. Violence begets violence. The second answer is the method of nonviolence resistance. This method became famous by Mohandas K. Gandhi and Dr. Martin Luther King, Jr. Gandhi made the method of nonviolent resistance famous in India when he used the method to free his country and the continent from the domination of the British Empire. Dr. King used the method of nonviolent resistance in Montgomery, Alabama to free 50,000 African Americans from the abuses of bus segregation.[59]

The module then moved to the presentation and question, "What is the method of nonviolent resistance for social justice?" This is not a method of cowardice or stagnant passivity. The nonviolent resister is not aggressive physically

---

[59] Ibid.

toward his/her opponent. However, the resister is constantly trying to persuade the opponent that he or she is mistaken. This method is aggressive spiritually. The belief is that the universe is on the side of justice. Nonviolent resistance does not seek to defeat or humiliate the opponent but to win friendship and understanding. The nonviolent resister uses non-cooperation and boycotts. The methods of resistance are not ends, but means to awaken shame within the opponent and connect the shame to the injustices in the community. Think about ways to awaken shame in your opponents. The end is redemption and reconciliation. The end of nonviolence resistance is the creation of the Beloved Community. The nonviolent resistance method is aimed at evil itself and not the persons caught in the forces of evil. In the Montgomery bus boycott, the tension was not between the races. The tension was between justice and injustice. The goal of the bus boycott was to defeat the injustice of the segregated bus service and not the people who were unjust. What are the injustices in your life and community? [60]

After presenting the questions and responses at the beginning of this segment of the module, the module then gave this directive, "Give your first reaction to the history and philosophy of the nonviolent method for social justice." Each participant responded in writing and discussed their reactions

---

[60] Ibid.

online with other citizens of the community. Then the module asked the question, "Can you identify or relate with the history and/or philosophy of this method for social justice? Why or Why not?" for each participant to respond. The next section discusses the second module for the Beloved Community Study Circle.

Beloved Community Study Circle Module Two

The second week of the online community began with a presentation and question, "What is the goal of the method of nonviolent resistance to social justice?" The goal of nonviolent resistance is the creation of the beloved community. At the center of nonviolence stands the principle of love. This love is not a sentimental and affectionate emotion. The love of the nonviolent method of resistance is to understand and to foster redeeming good will for all people. We are able to love the person who does the evil deed while hating the deed. [61]

Dr. King discovered that the most powerful weapon available to a voiceless and isolated people is the power of love as he studied Mahatma Gandhi's concept of *satyagraha* (*satya* is truth which equals love and *graha* is force). *Satyagraha* means love-force. The Christian doctrine of love operating

---

[61] Ibid.

through the Gandhian method of nonviolent resistance is a powerful tool as demonstrated in history.[62]

The module then moved to the presentation and question, "Why legislation, court orders, and executive decrees?" The law cannot change the heart but it restrains the heartless.[63] The nonviolent method understands that law only declares rights, but it cannot deliver rights.[64] Only people of action can hold the government accountable and give life to legislation, court orders, and executive decrees.[65]

Then the module moved to the presentation and question, "What is the American Dream?" The goal of nonviolent resistance is to bring into full realization the American Dream. The Dream is a place of social justice. The Dream is a place of equality of opportunity, privilege, and widely distributed property. The American Dream is a place of respect for the dignity and worth of human personality.[66]

---

[62] Martin Luther King Jr. *Strength to Love* (Philadelphia: Fortress Press, 1963), 151.

[63] Martin Luther King Jr. "An Address Before the National Press Club." *Congressional Record 108 (20 July 1962): 14247-49.*

[64] Ibid.

[65] Martin Luther King Jr. " The Case Against 'Tokenism'." *New York Times Magazine (5 August 1962): 11ff.*

[66] Martin Luther King Jr. "An Address Before the National Press Club." *Congressional Record 108 (20 July 1962): 14247-49.*

The American Dream calls for the recognition of the sacredness of human personality. The Declaration of Independence says, "All men are created equal. They are endowed by their Creator with certain inalienable rights among these are life, liberty, and the pursuit of happiness." The American Dream is a place of freedom for all people. Paul Tillich says, "Man is man because he is free." Tolstoy states, "I cannot conceive of a man not being free unless he is dead." The denial of freedom is a denial of life. Freedom is the capacity to deliberate, decide, and respond. Social injustice does not allow for freedom, and therefore it does not allow the American Dream.[67]

After presenting the questions and responses at the beginning of this module, the module gave this directive, "Give your first response to the theology of love, the creation of the Beloved Community and the role of law." The module posed the question, "Do you think the goals of the American Dream are possible? Why or Why not?" The participants responded by responding to the questions and participating in the online discussion. The next section discusses the third module for the Beloved Community Study Circle.

---

[67] Martin Luther King Jr. "The Ethical Demands for Integration." *Religion and Labor* *(May 1963): 1,3-4,7-8.*

Beloved Community Study Circle Module Three

Amendments to the Constitution

The third week of the online community began with the presentation of the thirteenth and fourteenth amendments of the Constitution. The following are sections one of the thirteenth and fourteenth amendments of the Constitution:

Thirteenth Amendment

Section 1. Neither slavery nor involuntary servitude, except as punishment for crime whereof the party shall have been duly convicted, shall exist within the United States, or any place subject to their jurisdiction.

Fourteenth Amendment

Section 1. All persons born or naturalized in the United States and subject to the jurisdiction thereof, are citizens of the United States and of the State wherein they reside. No State shall make or enforce any law which shall abridge the privileges or immunities of citizens of the United States; nor shall any State deprive any person of life, liberty, or property, without due process of law; nor deny to any person within its jurisdiction the equal protection of the laws.

Dred Scott v. Sanford

The module then moves to a presentation on landmark cases for online discussion. The first case is *Scott v. Sanford.* Dred Scott was born a slave in Virginia around 1799. In 1834, Dr. John Emerson, a surgeon in the U.S. army, bought Dred Scott in Missouri. After he purchased Scott, Emerson moved Scott to Illinois, a free state. In 1836, Scott and Emerson moved to present-day Minnesota. In the Missouri Compromise of 1820, Congress prohibited slavery in this Minnesota area. In 1838, Emerson and Scott moved back to Missouri. By this time Scott has a wife and two children. In 1843, Emerson died and left the ownership of Scott to his widow who lived in St. Louis, Missouri.[68]

Scott sued Mrs. Emerson for "false imprisonment" and battery. During this period, many slaves sued their masters and won their freedom after being taken to a free state. In 1857, the Superior Court of the United States found in favor of Sanford. They declared that African Americans are not citizens and thus do not have any rights.[69]

---

[68]Scott v. Sanford, 60 U.S. 393 (1857).

[69] Ibid.

In response to this case presentation, the module presents a directive stating, “Give your first response to the facts of the case and the decision of the case.”

Plessy v. Ferguson

The second landmark case presented in the module is *Plessy v. Ferguson.* In 1890, Louisiana passed a statute called the "Separate Car Act." The Act stated "that all railway companies carrying passengers in their coaches in this state, shall provide equal but separate accommodations for the white, and colored races, by providing two or more passenger coaches for each passenger train, or by dividing the passenger coaches by a partition so as to secure separate accommodations..." [70]

On June 7, 1892 Homer Plessy, a mixed race resident of Louisiana, purchased a first-class ticket on the East Louisiana Railway. Plessy was jailed when he sat in the "White" car and refused to move to the "Colored" car. Plessy argued the Separate Car Act violated the Thirteenth and Fourteenth Amendments to the Constitution. In 1896, the Supreme Court of the United States upheld the Louisiana State Supreme Court. The Court declared that the "Separate Car Act" was constitutional as long as there were separate but equal

[70] Plessy v. Ferguson, 163 U.S. 537 (1896).

accommodations.[71] In response to this case presentation, the module presented a directive, "Give your first response to the facts of the case and the decision of the case."

Brown v. Board of Education

The third landmark case presented in the module is *Brown v. Board of Education.* In the early 1950's Linda Brown, an African American student in Topeka, Kansas, applied to summer school. The Board of Education of Topeka denied her admission because of her race. A Kansas statute permitted cities of more than 15,000 people to maintain separate schools facilities based on race. The Browns sued the Board of Education of Topeka. The Browns argued that the segregated school system deprived the student of equal protection under the law as required under the Fourteenth Amendment. In 1954, the Supreme Court of the United States declared that segregated schools are "inherently unequal" and violate the Fourteenth Amendment.[72] In response to this case presentation, the module presented the directive stating, "Give your first response to the facts and decision of the case."

---

[71] Ibid.

[72] *Brown v. Board of Education*, 347 U.S. 483 (1954).

Miranda v. Arizona

The fourth landmark case presented in the module is *Miranda v. Arizona.* In 1963, Ernesto Miranda, a poor Mexican immigrant in Phoenix, Arizona was arrested and charged with rape and kidnapping. He was interrogated for two hours. The police officers did not inform Miranda of his Fifth Amendment right against self-incrimination or of his Sixth Amendment right to the assistance of a lawyer. During his trial, the prosecution used his confession to obtain a conviction. Miranda appealed the case. He argued that his confession should not be used in the case, because he was not informed of his rights. The United States Supreme Court declared that an individual held for interrogation must be informed of his or her right not to be compelled to self-incrimination and the right to consult with a lawyer to create admissible evidence. [73] In response to this case presentation, the module presented the directive, "Give your first response to the facts of the case and the decision of the case."

[73] *Miranda v. Arizona*, 384 U.S. 436 (1966).

The final section of the third module presented questions on the difference between treating people equal and the same. The first question in this section of the module asks, "Does treating people equally mean treating people the same? Why or why not?" Then the module moves to the next group of questions asking, "What does it mean to treat people equally in the following situations?" The following are the final questions for the module:

> 1. A man and a woman apply for the same job. What would the employer have to do to treat these two applicants equally?
>
> 2. Two patients come to the doctor with a headache. One patient has a basic headache and the other patient has a brain tumor. What would the doctor have to do to treat these patients equally?
>
> 3. Two students try to enter a school with stairs. One student is handicapped and the other is not. What would the school have to do to treat these two students equally?
>
> 4. A 12-year-old white student and a 12-year-old black student live in the same school district. What does the school district have to do to treat these two students equally?[74]

The next section discusses the fourth module for the Beloved Community Study Circle.

Beloved Community Study Circle Module Four

The fourth week of the online community began with the question, "What individual actions can you make today in your community as a change agent to address social injustice?" The first subsection of this section presented the question, "What two or three ideas seem most practical and useful?" The second subsection of this section presented the question, "What would it take to turn these ideas into reality?" The third subsection of this section presented the question, "What resources are in place that could help you turn your idea into reality?"

The module then moved to the second directive stating, "Provide a summary of your reactions and reflections to the issues and topics covered over the last four weeks."

Then the module progressed to question three, "What kind of public policy can help us with social injustices in our community?" The module then transitioned to the next question

---

[74] Street Law and Supreme Court Historical Society. "Landmark Supreme Court Cases," http://landmarkcases.org/plessy/equal_same.html (accessed March 25, 2005).

asking, “How can we create a beloved community? How can you as a change agent create a beloved community?”

The module concluded with the fifth directive and question, “Think about the personal or community experience with social injustice shared on the questionnaire at the beginning of the Study Circle, and based on what we have discussed over the last four weeks, how would you have addressed that situation?” The next section will provide the participants’ responses to the modules’ questions.

Chapter Four

THE FIELD EXPERIENCE

Creating a Beloved Community in West Virginia

Backgrounds of the Beloved Community Citizens

The Beloved Community Study Circle asked the community of Morgantown, West Virginia to face a critical issue—how to build a Beloved Community. The Study Circle asked the community of Morgantown to get involved in an online community discussion by examining Dr. Martin Luther King, Jr.'s teachings on the Beloved Community as a tool to address issues of social injustices in our community. There was an opportunity for people from all backgrounds and all parts of the community to participate in this constructive online conversation, and propose ways to build a Beloved Community.

The Beloved Community Study Circle selected ten applicants to participate in the Study Circle. Five of the ten participants completed the modules and exit surveys. The context associates, who helped with promoting the Study Circle and the researcher wanted to have more participants complete the program, but they were satisfied with the diversity of the participants and the diversity of their perspectives. The names used in this section are fictional. The participants were also identified as "citizens" of the Beloved Community.

The first participant, Jill Scott, is a thirty-five year old Black African Methodist Episcopal woman with more than twenty years of education. She wanted to participate in the Study Circle to share her experiences with injustices in various areas and stages of her life. She shares one story of social injustice in her questionnaire. The following is her story:

> While working in the academic setting, with over qualification for the position I held, the new manager felt as though my "color" was my only reason for having the position and that I had no knowledge to be in the position. This manager showed this opinion of me by refusing to acknowledge my presence in staff meetings and continually working opposite to set guidelines and protocols established for smooth project functionality. This led to several problems that I had to work extra hours to resolve.

The second participant, Tameka Jones, is a twenty-four year old Black African Methodist Episcopal woman with thirteen to sixteen years of education. She wanted to participate in the Study Circle in order to be involved in making the community a better place. She shares one story of social injustice in her questionnaire. The following is her story:

> When I was in elementary school, my brother and I were walking down the street and these guys in a truck called us 'niggers' and tried to run us over.

The third participant, Fernando Torres, is a thirty-seven year old Latino Catholic man with more than twenty years of education. He wanted to participate in the Study Circle because another participant invited him to participate and he believes "anything that expands his understanding of the world is always welcome." He shares one story of social justice in his questionnaire. The following is his story:

> Oh, please. It happens to me all the time just because I am Latino and do not speak English as a native speaker of the language. I was not served at a burger fast food restaurant. However, the person who came right behind me a couple of minutes later was helped. I said nothing. I just walked out and never returned to that particular store.

The fourth participant, Karen Smith, is a thirty-two year old Caucasian Methodist woman with thirteen to sixteen years of education. She wanted to participate in the Study Circle to learn how to identify social justice issues and their causes and learn what to do about it. She shares one story of social injustice in her questionnaire. The following is her story:

> My foster son came home from kindergarten with an assignment to build a rocket, but without the instruction sheet that all of the other children received. I immediately heard a tape of Chris Rock in my head saying, "Oh, I see. The BLACK boy comes home without the instructions. Can't a little brother be an astronaut?
>
> Of course, we made the rocket anyway, but I could not help but wonder about my interpretation of the event. Was the teacher racist? Was I racist for assuming that his lack of instructions had something to do with race and not some other problem? Certainly, this teacher's treatment of my foster son was unjust on several different occasions.
>
> Race may have been a factor. She may have assumed that it wasn't worth the trouble of trying to teach him, since he was from a broken home and had some behavior problems at the time.
>
> What I saw from her is that she was willing to completely give up on the child before he even had a chance to show what he is made of. To me, a person in authority giving a child less than what he needs and implying through

> actions that he doesn't count anyway is a grave injustice.

The fifth participant, Mary Hart, is a nineteen year old Caucasian Protestant woman with thirteen to sixteen years of education. She wanted to participate in the Study Circle in order to make a difference in Morgantown, West Virginia. She shares one story of social injustice in her questionnaire. The following is her story:

> Earlier this year I was harassed by my boyfriend's roommate. I reported the incident that night hours after it had happened. After the initial hearing he was told to move, which he refused to do. The residential director took no action for almost two months. He finally forced him to move after I called him. He never returned my phone call, and allowed two additional weeks for the kid to move. Harassment is serious, and it should be taken care of immediately. The director only forced the kid to move one building over, when most offenses result in leaving the campus or the university. I am extremely disappointed in the university's tolerance for delinquency. It is simply unacceptable. The community should show more support for tolerance and diversity and take more appropriate actions.

The next section will summarize the responses to the questions in module one.

Beloved Community Study Circle Module One

Tragedy of Slavery and Segregation

The system of slavery and segregation made African Americans feel inferior. This system of oppression scared the soul and distorted the personality of African Americans. This system gave the oppressor privileges and a false sense of superiority.

In response to these statements, the Study Circle began the online discussion with the question, "Do you agree with the statement on the tragedy of slavery and segregation? Why or why not?" Jill Scott agreed with the statement on the tragedy of slavery and segregation. She states that as a member of oppressed people, she still sees the evidence of this tragedy today. She states that there are still environments where someone of color has to work harder at the same task as their White counterpart and still not be seen as doing an excellent job. She believes a person of color can be over-qualified for a position and still not receive an interview. She states that there are too many examples to name as to why this tragedy is still going on today.

Tameka Jones agreed with the statement that slavery and segregation made African Americans feel inferior, and that it gave oppressors a false sense of privilege and superiority. She states that even though slavery has been abolished, many African Americans feel that Caucasian Americans still have the upper hand in life, and that they have to work twice as hard to get recognition when it comes to school and work.

Karen Smith agreed in part with the statement about the tragedy of slavery in America. She believes that in addition to giving slaveholders and non-blacks in general a false sense of superiority, the power these groups wielded over African Americans corrupted their souls and poisoned their personalities. Those abusing the power came to believe that abuse is power. She believes this worldview was not at all limited to the treatment of African Americans. She believes when one dehumanizes anyone it becomes much easier to dehumanize everyone, and the mental ability to depersonalize persons when the recognition of their human rights is inconvenient is a cultural habit that lives on to this day. She firmly believes that the legacies of family violence, child abuse, abortion, and a national hunger for war are symptoms of our country's early tolerance of intolerable violence.

Fernando Torres believes that any situation in which a person or group of people oppress others, the oppressed ones develop a sense of insecurity that diminishes their emotional and spiritual strength. He believes the oppressors usually use many strategies to remain in control. He states that some of those strategies include psychological torture and intimidation that result in the oppressed feeling inferior and completely fearful.

Fernando agreed with the statement on slavery and segregation. He states that slavery started out as a method to acquire cheap labor, but it eventually turned into white supremacy and the suppression of African Americans. He believes the government allowed slave owners to obtain that false sense of supremacy by not stepping in and taking a stand to proclaim that the constitutional and natural rights are for all human beings not just White men. Fernando believes this allowance created several outcomes. He believes African Americans learned to bond as a culture and work together, which can still be seen today. Fernando states that their progress has shown great strength; this strength should inspire all of us.

Fernando concludes his comments by stating that the majority of African Americans lived through hell on earth, but they didn't give up. He believes many White Americans still live with this falsity of supremacy unfortunately, which has been passed on from generation to generation. He also believes that it is really a shame that more hasn't been done to stop this level of oppression and discrimination. He understands that there are laws concerning affirmative action, but he is aware that some argue that affirmative action discriminates against the majority. Fernando states that he recognizes America is technologically and economically advanced, but he believes our cultural and ethnic attitudes are centuries behind. Fernando also recognizes that the economy of the agricultural South relied primarily on the African American work force and he knows that the South as a whole profited from the cheap labor, which made it extremely difficult to end slavery. Fernando knows that economy of the North pre-Civil War was based on factories, not agriculture. He reiterates the agricultural reality of the South at the end of his comments by discussing how extremely dependent the South was on the African American population and how the moral issue of slavery fought against wealth, money, and greed.

Philosophy of the Nonviolent Method for Social Justice.

The next session of the first module of the online community began with the presentation of the question, "How will the struggle against injustice be waged?" There are two responses to this question. The first answer is violence. Violence never solves social problems. Violence actually creates new problems. Violence begets violence. The second response is the method of nonviolence resistance made famous by Mohandas K. Gandhi and Dr. Martin Luther King, Jr.

Then after presenting the questions and responses at the beginning of this segment of the module, the module then gave the directive, "Give your first reaction to the history and philosophy of the nonviolent method for social justice." Each participant was to respond in writing and to discuss the question online with other citizens of the community.

Jill Scott states that she understands the history and philosophy of nonviolent resistance. She agreed that it is an effective form of resistance as history proves, but she also states that it is not an easy form of exacting change of social ills. She believes nonviolent resistance requires a sacrifice on the part of the resistor and a spiritual willingness to separate the evil of injustice from the person committing the injustice. This is why she believes that most injustices are most often met with forms of violence rather than nonviolence.

Tameka Jones believes that nonviolence is a powerful tool to use against injustices. She states that it takes more courage to be silent and stand your ground than it does to lash out against persecutors. She believes when you fight back against injustice with violence that you are just as bad as the persecutors.

Fernando Torres states that the nonviolent resistance method sounds unrealistic. This is Fernando's first reaction. He states that he knows in his heart that nonviolence resistance is the right method to solve conflict. He believes that he has applied it at times in his life. He does not see people learning to behave in this way. He believes the problem is not that the nonviolence resistance method is complicated because it is not, but people need to be educated and raised in that way of thinking from childhood. He knows this statement implies that society needs to raise an entire generation of nonviolent thinkers and wait until their descendants grow up thinking and feeling the same way.

Last night, he heard a story that involved nonviolence resistance. A Catholic person felt attacked when someone asked in Fernando's class, "What was the big deal with the death of the Pope?" Fernando stated that the Catholic person's reaction was calm but proactive, and the classmate explained in detail what the figure of the Pope meant to him and his Church. The classmate understood that the person who made the comment needed a better understanding and not an opposing reaction. Fernando stated that by explaining and helping her understand, the classmate used nonviolence resistance to persuade the other person and solve a "conflict" in a rational way.

Karen Smith states that effective nonviolent methods appeal to her because violence demands that people harden their hearts and cut off their compassion toward the people they are doing violence against. She states that history shows this generation, again and again, that people who fight injustice through violence may succeed in the short-term but eventually end up committing the same atrocities as those they fought against. She states that it is through committing acts of violence that people become able to inflict injustice without conscience. Karen believes nonviolent methods are like fighting fire with water instead of with more fire.

Mary Hart agrees with nonviolent resistance opposed to forcibly violent means. She believes violent measures are a waste of a nation's or a specific group's resources, not only materialistically, but also of the lives of young men and women. She states that communication is the key to a successful and just world. Mary believes more problems are created during the course of the war than are solved. She believes military personnel fight each other often over pride of their government, and the war does not stay between the militaries. It often spreads and causes civilian casualties and heartache. She could not say that war is unjustified; it is just time we take a different approach. Mary recognized that Gandhi's approach was successful by looking at his life and everything he accomplished. She believed he was an amazing man. She thinks nonviolence resistance is often misunderstood, because many people think non-violent resistance is for the weak, but it is truly for those who are the strongest.

Then the module posed the question, "Can you identify or relate with the history and or philosophy of this method for social justice? Why or why not?"

Jill Scott responded to this segment of the module. She states that she can identify with the philosophy of this method for social justice, but she knows that she could not react with nonviolence to social injustices if she did not have a spiritual foundation. She states that her human nature is to lash out and fight against injustices, "by any means necessary" to reach her determined goal. She believes with nonviolence there is a level of trust that your actions, while nonviolent, will get you to the same desired goal. She ends her comments by stating that this philosophy requires time and the results may take decades to see, but there are results as our history of nonviolent movements prove.

Tameka Jones responded to this segment by stating that she can relate to the history and philosophy of the nonviolence resistance movement because of two different experiences. When she was in elementary school, Dr. Martin Luther King, Jr.'s birthday was not a holiday in West Virginia. Her mother took her and her brother out of school on his birthday every year. She would take them to the Cultural Center and celebrate his birthday. Her mother along with other parents voiced to the staff of her elementary school that Dr. King's birthday should be honored for all the work he did.

Another time her family practiced a nonviolent resistance strategy was when she was in middle school. There was a tremendous amount of racial discrimination at her school from students as well as the staff. The parents of the few African American students that went to her school met at her grandmother's house to try to talk about what they could do to address the injustices at the school. Her mom got the attention of the local newspaper. The newspaper interviewed them about the stress of going to school and being threatened by other students based on the color of their skin. It was a nonviolent way to tell the community that they would not stand for injustice.

Fernando Torres is not completely sure of how much he personally can relate to this method. He knows in his heart that nonviolent resistance is the right method to solve conflict, but he does not see society at large learning to behave in this rational way. Fernando believes that people need to be educated and raised thinking and believing in pacifist ways to solve problems in their lives, because history has shown us that nonviolence resistance works. He believes that the Rev. Martin Luther King, Jr. and Mohandas Ghandi are two good examples, because they lived their lives convincing oppressors that their beliefs were wrong, and both men also showed them the right path to follow.

Fernando believes that all we need then is to persuade the rest of the world to follow the practices of nonviolence resistance. He states that we do not need to develop an extensive and expensive campaign to do that, but we can just tell our relatives and friends. He adds by saying that we can share with the closest ones in our lives this way of conflict resolution. He states that we can start making the world a better place for ourselves and for future generations by letting the Beloved Community be our start. He ends his comments by saying, "Now, go and tell it to the mountains."

Karen Smith states that she could relate to this history. She has found that being angry and confrontational with people who do injustices against her generally made matters worse. However, when she was able to find some way to relate to that person, she found some grain of compassion still left in her for them. When she began to see them as her brother or sister, things changed radically from that moment on.

Karen believes that love is miraculous, and finding a way to love someone who is being difficult to love, sets off a series of changes that she says she doesn't begin to understand. She has personally prayed for the power to not hate an individual, and two days later that individual would come to her and say, "I don't want to be like this anymore." Karen believes love is the source of our power as humans.

Mary Hart responded by discussing her involvement in the Institute for Human Dignity. The Institute is based on the idea of nonviolent resistance inspired by people like Gandhi and Nelson Mandela. She believes by uniting the voices of many people under specific causes, justice can be brought to the world. The next section discusses the responses of the citizens in the second module for the Beloved Community Study Circle.

Beloved Community Study Circle Module Two

The second week of the online community began with the presentation and question, "What is the goal of the method of nonviolent resistance for social justice?" The goal of nonviolent resistance is the creation of the Beloved Community. At the center of nonviolent stands the principle of love. This love is not sentimental and affectionate emotion. The love of the nonviolent method of resistance is to understand and to foster redeeming good will for all people. We are able to love the person who does the evil deed while hating the deed.

The module then transitioned to the presentation and question, "Why legislation, court orders, and executive decrees?" The law cannot change the heart but it restrains the heartless. The nonviolent method understands that law only declares rights but they cannot deliver the rights. Only the people of action can hold the government accountable and give life to legislation, court orders, and executive decrees.

Then the module moved to the presentation and question, "What is the American Dream?" The goal of the method of nonviolent resistance is to bring into full realization the American Dream. The Dream is a place of social justice. The Dream is also a place of equality of opportunity, privilege, and widely distributed property. The Dream is a place of respect for the dignity and worth of human personality. The Dream calls for a recognition of the sacredness of human personality.

The Declaration of Independence states that, "All men are created equal. They are endowed by their Creator with certain inalienable rights among these are life, liberty, and the pursuit of happiness." The American Dream is a place of freedom for all people. Paul Tillich says, "Man is man because he is free." Tolstoy states, "I cannot conceive of a man not being free unless he is dead." The denial of freedom is a denial of life. Freedom is the capacity to deliberate, decide, and respond. Social injustice does not allow for freedom and therefore the American Dream.

After presenting the questions and responses at the beginning of this module, the module gave this directive, "Give your first response to the theology of love, the creation of the Beloved Community and the role of law."

Jill Scott believes this theology of love has a biblical basis, because the only way one can truly hate the evil act and not the person performing the act is to love the person as God would love the person. She believes this is a struggle that we all go through and our belief in this theology or our buy in of this theology is based on how we ultimately define love. She believes if one defines love as an emotional or affectionate action, the separation of the act from the person is not possible, but if one defines it as part of a higher calling of equality, the separation of the action from the actor becomes clear.

Jill states that this clarity of definition helps to lead to the creation of a Beloved Community, for the treatment of its members would be first and foremost be equal – without bias, for in a Beloved Community every person has the same worth. She believes that with each person holding the same worth and importance, the role of law then becomes clear as well, for the statues that are set forth are simple to uphold as there is no need for reinterpretation based on a persons worth or place in society.

Tameka Jones believes the theology of love is to love a person who does evil and hate the deed is not an impossible task. However, she believes as humans we tend to change the way we act according to the setting. At this point in her response, Tameka gives an example. She states that a mother of a two year old disciplines her daughter, and the daughter tells her mother, "I hate you!" Tameka says that the mother realizes that the child is responding in that way because she cannot have her way. According to Tameka, the mother loves the child, but hates the particular behavior of the child. The child will eventually tell the mother, "I love you," again after time has passed. Tameka ends her comments by saying that it is more difficult for us to use the same principles in similar situations.

Tameka says that forgiving a family member may be more easily accepted than forgiving a coworker or someone else, because we forget to separate the person from the behavior. She believes the creation of a Beloved Community is possible, but it will take time, compassion, and understanding. She also believes that the law is just a piece of paper unless people put it into action. She agrees that it cannot change a person's heart, but it does provide a form of restraint from misconduct. Tameka believes that if people do not use the law to help bring social justice to past, then it is useless. Tameka knows that often people perish due to their lack of knowledge.

Fernando Torres believes the theology of love at the core of nonviolence resistance is the answer to the world's problems. He states that if we all learn to understand and distinguish between evil deeds and people, it would be easier to forgive and forget. However, he believes the question lies in whether or not we can separate the evildoers from their evil deeds. Fernando believes the historical Jesus gave us many examples throughout his life. He always forgave evildoers and sinners, condemning the sin and the evil deeds they performed.

In our daily lives, nevertheless, Fernando believes we find it hard to forgive; we hold grudges for insignificant things, let alone really significant things. He states that the difficulty in seeing the evil deed and the person as separate lies in the obvious fact that the person is the performer of the evil. Fernando says, "Perhaps if we recognize that we are only human, that we all make mistakes, and that it is better to host love in our hearts rather than hate and grudges, we will live more peacefully." He believes that we need to let go of bad memories and move on.

Karen Smith believes that love is the only thing that really works in the long term. She consciously chose to believe that love in action could eventually crowd out the evil that is so pervasive in the world. She believes that the project of changing the world into a loving environment that allows freedom for all is a multigenerational task. She adds that it is unlikely that everyone is just going to become decent tomorrow. But she doesn't need them to become decent tomorrow. She believes that everyone is given a certain sphere of influence and a certain territory of opportunities to love. Karen believes that each act of love changes one person's experience and empowers that person to choose love in their sphere of influence, and in this way, pockets of love and justice can grow until they grow into and merge with other growing pockets of love. She tells "evil" to watch out because it does not have any place to go. She ends her comments by saying that only free individuals can create a loving world by the big and small choices that they make everyday.

Mary Hart believes the theology of love goes beyond understanding and redeeming good will for everyone. A loving person and the Beloved Community will go beyond the theology of love and bring love into action. We may not understand why certain injustices occur, but we know why we must fight against them. For example, She does not understand how money, especially to the point of extreme wealth, can cause people to enslave their own kind and take away their natural rights and continue to profit as demonstrated in slavery. She is reminded of the following Corinthian doctrine:

> Love is patient, love is kind. It does not envy, it does not boast, it is not proud. It is not rude, it is not self-seeking, it is not easily angered, it keeps no record of wrongs. Love does not delight in evil but rejoices in the truth. It always protects, always trusts, always hopes, and always perseveres. Love never fails.[75]

[75] I Corinthians 13:4-8.

Mary believes that it is through compassion that the evildoer can be touched, not through physical violence.

Mary also believes the concept of the Beloved Community is simply wonderful. She thinks it seems more of a nirvana, but it is something we should all work together to strive for the manifestation of the Beloved Community. She believes that a community based on love, compassion, and the will to act in love would truly be able to reach out and touch the world. She would love to be a part of such a community, and most other people would agree. She understands that it wouldn't be perfect, but the way this community solved issues and interacted would be different from anything seen today. Mary believes many people would be attracted to this community. She believes the Beloved Community is a worthy goal.

Mary adds that the idea of the law not enforcing rights makes the law seem inadequate. She states that for the law to only declare the rights shows its weakness and the weakness of the people. She believes that whatever the law declares, they should be able to enforce. Otherwise, she didn't see the point of the law. Mary believes that the people have given the government the power to make these legislations. She believes that it is their fault if they are not enforced properly. Mary believes people should have their own standards that need not be enforced, and the standards of both the people and the law should be parallel and inseparable.

Then the module examined the question, "Do you think the goals of the American Dream are possible? Why or why not?" for the participants to respond in writing and discuss online.

Jill Scott believes the goals of the American Dream are noble ones, but the attainment of the Dream is another story all together. She thought that the American Dream could be obtained and that was a possible pursuit, but the hearts of the people are not in a place to make the Dream a reality. She believes that the lack of respect for others, the oppression of those different from us, the mistreatment of the less fortunate, and the "every man for themselves" mentality has made the Dream impossible. She closes her response by stating that all of these things are hindrances to the American Dream and without love she doesn't see the Dream becoming a reality.

Tameka Jones believes that the American Dream is possible but we have to fight for that Dream. She believes that equality of opportunity, privilege, and property came to minorities, but they had to fight for that Dream. Even though there are more opportunities now, Tameka states that there is still a great deal of subtle social injustices occurring everyday. She believes it takes hard work on everyone's behalf to make the American Dream come to past.

Fernando Torres states that "life, liberty and the pursuit of happiness" are inalienable rights given to us by God and by the Constitution. However, he believes that the lack of socioeconomic equality keeps us from reaching those goals, especially the last one, pursuit of happiness. Fernando asks, “How could one be happy if his or her life is full of restlessness due to financial constraints?” He is not saying that money is everything, or that it equals happiness, but he believes that we cannot pretend that the head of a household where basic needs are not met because of the lack of money is a happy person, especially if they struggle everyday to bring food to the table, pay bills, find a job, etc. Fernando believes that is the reality of many American families and for those people, the American Dream is nearly impossible. Fernando states that history has shown us that perseverance, strength, and courage are all one needs to reach this utopia, the Dream.

Fernando invited us to look at the actor turned politician, Arnold Schwarzenegger. Fernando stated that he came to America as an athlete, but was able to accomplish much more than what he originally planned for his life, just with perseverance, physical and spiritual strength, and courage. Fernando believes Schwarzenegger set his mind on specific goals, and all he did was strive to reach them. Fernando believes Schwarzenegger is sure that the American Dream exists, and that it is reachable. Perhaps, this Dream exists, but

Fernando believes it eludes some. Fernando believes that as long as the entire system does not recognize every single person as equal to the rest, there will not be an American Dream for everyone. Fernando believes social justice is first in this case.

Karen Smith believes that the goals of the American Dream are not only possible, but also inevitable. She states that this is a hard choice that she makes everyday in the face of the evidence of humanity's failure to love. She says, "I'm only able to believe this through the knowledge that God's power is unlimited and can redeem even us, even here, even now." Karen states that she knows that God's love is the only ultimate reality, and in the end God always wins. She states that this is the closest she can come to for any sense of optimism about the human condition.

Mary Hart does not think the American Dream is completely possible. She believes there are too many people trying to get ahead in life by participating in social injustices for the American Dream to be successful. She believes that there are always people who do not care about others. In a perfect world, Mary believes that the American Dream would be easily obtainable. However, Mary believes the American Dream is definitely a cause to pursue. She believes that everyone deserves the same opportunities, the same inalienable rights, and the same respect. She adds to her comments by stating that until every man, woman, and child are willing to change, she believes the American Dream will be impossible to achieve. She also believes life would be so much more fulfilling when all are free to pursue their dreams without the common impediments of social injustices. She states that in an environment of social justice, either the people must be committed to the cause or some group must have the authority and power to enforce social justice.

Mary recognizes that society is primarily based on merit. She demonstrates this fact by asking and responding to a question, "Does a doctor, one who saves the lives of others and has completed at least eight years of higher education, deserve the same amount of property as a music video director who never made it through high school?" Mary agrees that property should be distributed, but to a degree.

In our society, Mary believes that people must be rewarded for their work. She knows it is unfair to give the same accreditations to people of different professions. She understands that if our society comes to this, why should the person wanting to be the doctor even be motivated to finish high school, let alone complete the rigorous medical school curriculum if he or she is rewarded the same as everyone else? She's not saying people should be deprived from this property distribution, but there still must be some sort of consideration set for those hard working and motivated individuals. But, as of right now, Mary believes the American Dream is a belief of our dreams. The next section discusses the responses of the citizens in the third module for the Beloved Community Study Circle.

Beloved Community Study Circle Module Three

Amendments to the Constitution

The third week of the online community began with the presentation of the thirteenth and fourteenth amendments of the Constitution. The module then moved to a presentation on landmark cases for the online discussion. The first landmark case discussed presented in the module is *Scott v. Sanford.* In response to this case presentation, the module presented a directive stating, "Give your first response to the facts and decision of the case."

Jill Scott states that the ruling was incorrect, because Scott was born in the U.S. He was a U.S. citizen with said rights according to that Amendment of the Constitution.

Tameka Jones states that the ruling was unconstitutional. She states that when Dred Scott and Dr. Emerson moved to Illinois, a free state, Dred Scott should have been freed from slavery.

Fernando Torres states that the fact that Black people were not considered citizens and had no rights was morally wrong. He believes that the law should follow minimum moral values of respect and equality. He states that the Constitution makes us all equal under the law. Therefore, Fernando believes the ruling was wrong.

Karen Smith states that it is really hard to have a response to something so "patently absurd." She believes that the courts of law entertaining any arguments based on one person's right to own another person makes a mockery of justice. Karen believes the court came to a ridiculous conclusion, because the arguments were based on false premises, i.e. that some persons are persons and some are not.

Mary Hart believes the courts ruled incorrectly on the case as well. First, she states that the Constitution states that "all men are created equal" and have "certain unalienable rights" including "life, liberty, and the pursuit of happiness." Therefore, Mary believes that slavery is a violation of these God given rights. Mary states that by law, upon moving to Illinois, Dred Scott was free. She believes that from there on, it should have been his choice to exercise his freedom or choose to remain serving the family. Mary states that even if he had chosen to continue to serve the family, Scott would have still been considered free along with his family. She believes that once a man is free, he is free forever, and this is not contingent on where he lives.

Mary believes that upon moving back to Missouri, Scott is still free. She states that Emerson had no legal right to transfer the ownership of Scott and his family to his wife, when he did not legally own the Scott family anymore. Scott had every right to sue. However, Mary is not sure why Scott waited until Dr. Emerson died to pursue legal action. Mary concludes her comments by stating that the Superior Court ruled incorrectly; the verdict was unconstitutional, because African Americans are equal to Euro-Americans, and they always have been. Mary concludes her comments by stating that African Americans were indeed citizens, and they possess every natural right.

The second landmark case presented in the module is *Plessy v. Ferguson.* In response to this case presentation, the module presented the directive stating, "Give your first response to the facts of the case and the decision of the case."

Jill Scott sees this case as an example of a state making a law that abridged the privileges of Mr. Plessy. She believes that Mr. Plessy's claim that the state law was unconstitutional is correct. Jill adds that the fact that Mr. Plessy was of mixed race, the way that states law read, he could in fact choose where he wanted to sit. She believes he was within his right to be in the "White Only" car.

Tameka Jones states that if a particular race can only sit in a certain coach then there is no equality. Tameka states that in *Plessy v. Ferguson*, the court declared that the "Separate Car Act" was constitutional as long as there were separate but equal accommodations. Tameka believes the "Separate Car Act" itself was the opposite of what the Fourteenth Amendment of the Constitution states, "No state shall make or enforce any law which shall abridge the privileges or immunities of citizens of the United States; Nor shall any State deprive any person of life, liberty, or property without due process of law..." Tameka states that the word liberty can be defined as the condition of being free from restriction or control. Therefore, Tameka believes that the "Separate Car Act" was restrictive because the passenger coaches separated by race and either a partition or a separate coach.

Fernando Torres states that based on his knowledge of the law in this case, the decision of the court was right. However, he states that if there were not real "equal" accommodations for both White and Colored people, then the Court's ruling is wrong.

Karen Smith states that the cases just get sillier and sillier. She states that again we have courts making decisions based on nonexistent concepts, i.e. that the physical separation of the races is an issue of interest to the law and not simply an arbitrary habit of some folks who happened to have had the power to enforce it at one time. Karen believes the premise that the different races are really that different was adequately disproved by the existence of Mr. Plessy himself.

Karen makes a statement by asking, "If the differences we see between populations reflected any actual, biological reality, how is it that we mix with such ease?" Karen believes power was the only issue that the court considered – the power to define people out of their God given rights and constitutional protections. Karen closes her statement by describing this abuse of power as "ridiculous."

Mary Hart believes separate is not equal. She states that as long as there is separation, very few people are going to consider that as equal. She believes that as long as White men are separated from Black men, they are still going to engender feelings of supremacy. Mary believes that in no way is segregation equality. She believes that those railroad companies cannot guarantee that the separate accommodations are equal. Therefore, Mary believes that the only way equality can be established is through integration. She states that all citizens whether Black or White should be treated equally in all matters. Mary believes segregation is unconstitutional, because it was unconstitutional of the parties involved to deny Mr. Plessy a seat where he chose. Mary believes that the courts ruled incorrectly again and in violation of the constitution.

The third landmark case presented in the module is *Brown v. Board of Education.* In response to this case presentation, the module presented the directive stating, "Give your first response to the facts of the case and the decision of the case."

Jill Scott states that this case is one where the law was actually upheld and ultimately changed the course of this nation. Jill states that the school's ability to deny a student an education based upon their race was unconstitutional and was "inherently unequal" treatment for that student who was by birth a US citizen and by right should not be denied the rights of their citizenship.

Tameka Jones states that in *Brown v. Board of Education,* the Browns sued the Board of Education of Topeka because a Kansas statue permitted cities of more than 15,000 people to maintain separate schools facilities based on race. Therefore, Linda Brown an African American was denied admission to summer school. The Supreme Court of the United States declared that segregated schools are "inherently unequal" and violate the Fourteenth Amendment. Tameka believes this was a landmark case, because it showed that separate but equal is not equal. She agrees with the decision of this case.

Fernando Torres states that we all know the court was right in this case. Fernando states that segregation is wrong because it promotes inequality.

Karen Smith states that finally the words "inherently unequal" are being used sensibly. She believes that this decision represents a step in the right direction. Karen thinks it is staggering that it took so long.

Mary Hart believes the Supreme Court ruled in line with the Constitution. She states that the courts finally agreed that segregation is not equal. Mary believed that Linda Brown had every right to be educated at the school of her choice, because the Constitution should not discriminate between races. She states that all men, women, and children are equal under it. Mary acknowledges that the Constitution was not written with regard to race, but she believes it was about time that the Supreme Court ruled with the correct interpretation of the Constitution.

The fourth landmark case presented in the module is *Miranda v. Arizona.* In response to this case presentation, the module presented the directive stating, "Give your first response to the facts of the case and the decision of the case."

Jill Scott believes the confession should not be used because Ernesto was not given the proper information concerning his rights nor was he given the opportunity to consult a lawyer.

Tameka Jones' response was based on the fact that Ernesto was convicted of rape and kidnapping as a result of his confession. Tameka states that whether he was guilty or not, according to the law, he was not informed of his rights and was unable to consult a lawyer, his conviction was unconstitutional.

Fernando Torres states that this is a very clear example of how complicated our legal system has become, and how it can be manipulated. Fernando states that the facts provided do not tell us whether or not Mr. Miranda understood English, or if he knew the United States Constitution. Nevertheless, in the appeal he uses the Fifth and the Sixth Amendments to get an acquittal. Fernando does not know whether he was actually guilty of the crimes for which he was arrested. Fernando realizes that if it were not for this case, we would not know today what rights we have when we are faced with the police and an arrest order.

Karen Smith states that she does not have very strong feelings about this case. She believes we should all be aware of our own rights and not wait for the government to grant them to us or tell us what they are. However, she can identify with Mr. Miranda's plight. She believes he probably feared that the police would kill him if he did not play along. From that perspective, she believes requiring the police to state each individual's rights as they are taken into custody does serve to remind the police of the standard to which they must hold their behavior. In other words, she knows what her rights are, and the police better know what they are too.

Mary Hart states that the Miranda Rights must be read to all people before interrogation. She believes that most people are read their Miranda Rights the moment they are arrested, because the reading of rights is protocol. She understands that as a citizen in the United States, people are considered innocent until proven guilty, and every person maintains all their rights until proven guilty, including the reading of the Miranda Rights. She believes that in the majority of cases, there is enough available evidence outside the confession to convict the defendant if they are truly guilty. Mary believes the police need to treat arrestees as full citizens with all of their rights. She believes that the police in this situation should have known better than to not read Mr. Miranda his rights. Mary concluded her comments by stating that the police stepped out of their boundaries, and they should take full responsibility for their mistake.

The final section of the third module presented questions on the difference between treating people equal versus the same.

Jill Scott believes that equal treatment does mean treating people equally no matter the standing of the person. She also believes, with respect to the law, all persons should receive the same treatment.

Tameka Jones believes that treating people equally means treating people the same in the context given. For example, in the context of school, she states that students should be treated equally. She believes that if there is a student who has been diagnosed with a learning disability, then that student should be able to have the accommodations necessary to learn the same things as students without learning disabilities. An example of a different context is an emergency department of a hospital. Patients are admitted and are seen according to the severity of their problem. In this situation, Tameka believes that the equality of patients' treatment is based on which patient's problem is the most life threatening. According to Tameka, a person who had a lung punctured in a car accident will be seen before the person who has a sprained ankle.

Fernando Torres believes treating people the same does not guarantee that they have the same opportunities. For instance, he has been treated politely by his professors, but he has also found out that Caucasians in the same class have received "concessions" in the form of extension dates for submitting assignments. He states that this is totally wrong. Fernando believes that treating people "equally" means giving everyone the same type and amount of opportunities for everything.

Karen Smith believes equality means equality of opportunity, not equality of outcome. She believes that if one person is dangerous, take proper precautions. However, she states that we cannot lock up the whole nation in the interest of equality just because there are dangerous people. She believes equality means that everyone gets the same opportunities. She thinks each individual should decide what they will do with that opportunity, and each of us will live with the results of our own free choices.

Mary Hart believes treating people equally does mean treating them the same. She believes Americans are all equal; they are given all the same natural and basic rights in the Constitution. Therefore, equality is sameness. She believes one cannot have equality in segregation, because there is nothing equal about segregation. Mary believes that people must have the same opportunities to be equal.

Mary adds that all people are free; no one is enslaved to other men in America anymore. She believes we are all the same on that level. Mary believes that we all have the right to attend any school regardless of race. She states, "In equality, race is not an impediment; race is invisible." She also believes that we have equal opportunity employers to ensure companies are treating all people equally, the same. She states that all people are given the same employment opportunity based on credentials not skin color, and we have Affirmative Action to ensure that race is not a credential for acceptance. Mary believes that ethnicity should be invisible if not embraced. She ends her comments by stating that equality does mean treating all people the same.

Then the module moves to the next group of questions asking, "What does it mean to treat people equally in the following situations?" The following are the questions in this section of the module:

1. A man and a woman apply for the same job. What would the employer have to do to treat these two applicants equally?

2. Two patients come to the doctor with a headache. One patient has a basic headache and the other patient has a brain tumor. What would the doctor have to do to treat these patients equally?

3. Two students try to enter a school with stairs. One student is handicapped and the other is not. What would the school have to do to treat these two students equally?

4. A 12-year-old white student and a 12-year-old black student live in the same school district. What does the school district have to do to treat these two students equally?

In the next section, the citizens of the Beloved Community respond to these questions.

Jill Scott states that the employer would need to look solely at the person's qualifications for the position and not their gender in response to the first question. In response to the second question, she states that due to the severity of one person's injury, the doctor would have to treat based on the level of importance. In response to the third question, she states that the school should have provided alternate access for those students that are not physically able to use certain facilities. She believes that this gives both students the same opportunity to equally access the same school. In response to the fourth question, she states that both students would have access to the same education.

Tameka Jones states that in order for a man and woman who applied for the same job to be treated equally, the employer will make the decision of who will be hired based on their credentials and interviews in response to the first question. In response to question two, she states that in order for the doctor to treat the two patients equally, the doctor will treat each patient according to the policy and procedure of treating each condition. The policies for treating a brain tumor and a basic headache are different, but Tameka believes that as long as the doctor follows the proper steps of treatment for each patient according to the patient's diagnosis, the patients will get equal treatment. In response to the third question, she states that in order for the two students to have equal treatment in school, the school must provide means for the handicapped child to get upstairs by providing an elevator or chair lift. In response to the fourth question, she states that in order for the White and Black student living in the same school district to be treated equally, they must be provided with the same opportunities. She ends her comments with stating that the children need to ride the same school bus, have the same textbooks, etc.

Fernando Torres states that along with the posting for the position, the employer must announce the procedures and methods used for the final selection in response to the first question. He states that each candidate, regardless of his or her gender and race, should be treated following those guidelines word by word. In response to question two, he states that because the patients have exactly the same symptoms, the doctor will have to perform exactly the same tests and procedures to diagnose both patients. In response to question three, he states that the school needs to build the school in such a way that everyone can have access to the building and services they offer. In response to question four, Fernando states that both students must have the same opportunities to attend school, including accommodations in and access to the school and all its services.

Karen Smith states that the employer must carefully consider the candidates' qualifications and experience in response to question one. In response to question two, she states that the doctor should treat the patients' respective causes of their disorders, not merely the symptoms. In response to question three, she states the school should build the school so that both students can navigate it independently. Finally, in response to question four, she states that the school should teach both students equally with the same level of devotion and hold them both to the same ethical and behavioral standards.

Mary Hart states that the employer should base the application process strictly on credentials and not on the gender factor in response to question one. She states that the employer can compare education, experience, character, references, and numerous other aspects of the applicants to ensure the best person is chosen for the job. In response to question two, she states that the doctor would have to see and treat both patients to treat them equally. However, she believes triage must be considered if both patients were in the emergency setting. In an office setting, the doctor would give them the same amount of time and consideration.

In response to question three, she states that the school would have to provide both students with a means to getting to higher floors. She states that the stairs would suit the student without a disability, and a ramp or an elevator would suit the student with a disability. However, she suggests that the elevator and ramp could suit both students. Finally, in response to question four, she states that the school district must provide both students with a quality education. Mary believes that both students must have access to the same teachers, classmates, and subjects, and both students must be given the same educational and physical opportunities. She states that there can't be any bias or preference shown toward one student or the other, because both must be punished and rewarded the same. The next section discusses the fourth module for the Beloved Community Study Circle.

Beloved Community Study Circle Module Four

The fourth and final week of the online community began with the question, "What individual actions can you take today in your community as an agent of change to address social injustice?" The first subsection of this section presented the question, "What two or three ideas seem most practical and useful?" The second subsection of this section presented the question, "What would it take to turn these ideas into reality?" The third subsection of this section presented the question, "What resources are already in place that could help you turn your idea into reality?" The citizens of the Beloved Community responded to these questions during the fourth week of the Study Circle.

Tameka Jones thinks one step that she can take today in order to move toward a Beloved Community is to learn about the laws concerning social injustices. She believes a basic understanding of some of these laws will help her to be able to plead the case in an intelligent manner. Another individual action she states that she could do is to lead a forum concerning social injustices to get an idea about how the community feels and maybe get insight into the reasons why people hate. Secondly, the library, internet, and local government are great tools to learn about laws concerning social injustices. She believes the forum would also be useful to learn about laws concerning social injustices. Thirdly, she believes in order to make the reality of learning about laws is simply a matter of taking time to do the research. She states a forum, on the other hand, would require more work, but the most important job would be to promote the forum. Tameka states that the resources for such programs are churches and colleges, because both institutions are a means for communicating information for the development of our community.

Fernando Torres states that the first thing that comes to his mind is obviously to take action. If he sees or finds out about any social injustice that is being committed against any of my friends, he will raise his voice and express his disapproval. But more than that, he will encourage others to allow themselves to be heard.

Karen Smith states that she can make herself remain compassionate towards individuals who commit injustice. She can call an injustice an injustice when she sees it. She believes she can raise her children to hate the sin while loving the sinner. She states that she can educate others in her immediate sphere of influence about the injustices she sees. In the long term, she believes raising her children to be intolerant of wrongdoing, yet tolerant of people's frailties is probably the most practical she says she can do on a daily basis. Also, she believes refusing to shut up and accept injustice will keep the spotlight on the issues. Secondly, she states that she must assess and address her emotional state to stay loving. When her compassion runs low, she prays. It is an ongoing process. Finally, Karen states that God is a constant resource. It is going to take a miracle to eradicate injustice and abuses of power.

Mary Hart states that a voice will be the key to changing social injustice. She believes that it is important for social injustices to be brought to the surface, out and in the open, and publicized, whether it is one voice standing alone or a group of voices crying out together. She believes the public must be informed about how prevalent social injustices are in today's society. Mary believes that people need to be shown the steps for creating justice. She adds that the voice representing social justice needs to give the general public the opportunity to be a part of the change and make a difference on an individual level. Once the public is aware of and supports the issue, it can be brought to the attention of higher levels, such as the school board or the city council and working its way up to the state, national, and international level. Once the right people are aware of the issue, they can invent the creative tension needed to demand change.

She states that when a person sees an act of injustice, it is important to stand up for your beliefs, morals, and justice. Mary believes that by not standing up for justice, one is saying justice is not necessary. She states that people need to stand up, speak, and act for social justice. Mary believes that leading by actions is the most important step of all. She believes that if a person is seen supporting what they verbally say, more people are apt to follow them. She believes that working with a community, church, or university organization can act as an agent for change, because often they will already have the funds and support one would need. Mary states that involvement is also crucial in addressing social injustice. She believes that once joining a group, you should be active in it, because it would not take much effort at all to turn these ideas of justice into reality. She believes that the most influential ways are already in place. Mary closes her comments by stating that people just need to take the initiative to join a group and share their interests.

The module then shifted to the directive stating, "Provide a summary of your reactions and reflections to the issues and topics covered over the last four weeks." Then the module moved to the question asking, "What kind of public policy can help us with social injustices in our community?" The module then moved to the next question asking, " How can you as a change agent create a Beloved Community? Then the module ends with one final question. The following is the final question answered by the citizens: "Think about your experience with social injustice shared on the questionnaire at the beginning of the Study Circle. Based on what we have discussed over the last four weeks, how would you have addressed that situation?"

Tameka Jones states that after reflecting on the questions and answers of people participating in the discussion, it can be agreed that people want a Beloved Community. However, she believes that in order for this to come to past people must be willing to speak against social injustices in a nonviolent manner. Tameka believes a public policy that could help us with the social injustices in the community is a "zero tolerance" policy on social injustices. She advocates fines and educational requirements for breaking the zero tolerance policy could be implemented. Over the past four weeks, she has learned the definitions for a Beloved Community and the nonviolent resistance method. Reading some of the outcomes of the court cases made her angry. However she realized that you must love the person and hate the behavior. She now understands that if you combat social injustices with hate then more hate will be produced. She believes that if you combat social injustices with love then peaceful resolutions are produced.

After finishing all the questions for the Beloved Community Study Circle, Tameka believes that she has learned a few things. First, she learned that many people who act out in hate simply do not know the truth. She believes that there are two situations that may occur. The first is that people hate, because they were taught to hate. Tameka thinks these people probably don't even really understand what they are saying. She states that they just call people derogatory names, but they may not even know what those words mean. With this group of people, she believes that we have to teach them the truth. She states that the other set of people may have a problem with generalizing attributes about people as a result of one bad experience with someone of a different race, gender, socioeconomic status, etc., and believe that everyone else of that race, gender, socioeconomic status, etc. is the same. Therefore, Tameka believes that this person walks around with a delusion of the attributes of certain people. Regardless of why people hate, Tameka believes that we must first help people understand that their hate is purposeless, and then we must teach them the truth. Tameka believes the truth is that everyone is created equal and has a right to live a happy and peaceful life.

In conclusion, as Tameka thinks back on the social injustices that she experienced in the past, some of the situations she would have addressed the same, other ones she would have done something differently. She thinks she would have questioned some people who made statements like "You talk like you are White," or people that called her a "nigger." She is led to believe that if she had asked these people to explain themselves, they would not have anything to say. She believes that often people say things that they hear, but have no basis. She now believes this is the time when she could teach people the truth.

Fernando Torres states that the two things that stick to his mind are the legal issues and the notion of nonviolence resistance presented in the modules. As for the first issue, he sums it up as a very good thing that has happened in America and that is the new laws that protect and guarantee equal rights for everyone. However, Fernando thinks our society could be better today if those legal initiatives had been taken on earlier in the past century. As for the nonviolent resistance method to fight social injustice, he says that history has shown us (with examples such as Ghandi and Christ) that nonviolence prevails at the end. He believes that there is no need to be physically aggressive to protest and express your point of view. However, he believes that we need law enforcement agents who really take their job seriously and take care of social injustices in our community, because there are plenty of equality laws already. He believes that we need to educate people to respect those laws and have local authorities enforce those laws.

Fernando believes the creation of the Beloved Community actually takes little effort. He believes that we just need to live our lives following the examples found in the Judeo-Christian tradition: do no harm to others, help as many as you can when they need it, and treasure life in all forms. Also, we should teach others to live this way, but not necessarily preaching. He believes our example should suffice.

In conclusion, as he thinks about his past experience of being discriminated against in a fast food restaurant when he was not served and simply walked away, Fernando states he was really angry inside and still to this day he does not go to that place. However, given what he learned in the Beloved Community Study Circle, he thinks he acted in the right way, and he does not think he could act differently. He states that if he had the chance to go back to that situation, he would have written a letter to the local paper and or filed a complaint with the manager, but he still believes his actions represented nonviolence resistance.

Karen Smith states that she had to work very hard not to give into the depression and hopelessness when she reflects on human history and face the depth of humankind's depravity. She believes that even small contributions, such as her own, have the power to change the human experience.

Karen keeps feeling that she has used the website ineffectively or that she has missed some vital information, because she doesn't feel like she has any more tools for bringing people into a sensible relationship with each other than she had before. However, she is very excited to read the responses of the other Study Circle participants to see what they got that she missed. She is also grateful that she lives in a time when there are at least some people who see the work of equality, human dignity, and justice as important enough to study.

Karen thinks our constitutional right to free speech is the only way the government can help or even allow us to address injustices. She has given up on government intervention. She believes that public policy is always in the hands of those who have power already. She believes that the issues of injustice primarily impact those of us who don't have power. She also believes that the actions of contentious individuals keep the policy makers in line. However, she believes that we must retain our right to free speech if we are to blow the whistle on abuses of power and bring about a public demand for fairness.

Finally, she knows that she must love. In particular, she states that she must love and spend time with people who appear to be different from her. This is difficult for her to do. She states that she doesn't see a lot of clansmen or hookers, for example, on her street, where she works, or at her church. She states she must find ways to make herself available to people with these and other kinds of problems. She has found that no matter how strange a person seems, if she can spend enough time with them to look them in the eyes, then true connection and compassion can move between them. So, she decided she must create a Beloved Community by going where the pain is and loving those people with their pains. When people stop hurting, they stop hurting others. She said that she must go to the Nazi and love him, and she knows this is not a small task.

In conclusion, Karen states that she can see with all of this reflection under her belt that while she did not react aggressively to her son's teacher on the outside, her internal reaction was one of anger and extreme judgment. While her awareness made her able to move around the injustice, she really did nothing to heal it. Now when she encounters such a situation in the future, she states that she will be conscious enough of her internal reaction to pray out the anger and judgment. Then she will pray for healing, clarity, love, and grace for the individual who commits the injustice. If she feels prompted and capable, she stated that she will try to discuss the situation with the offender. She thinks this is really the hard part.

In the past, when Karen tried to reason with people who behave unreasonably, her judgment and anger contaminated the communication. She questions her own ability to reach out in love and with the right spirit in such circumstances. However, if that is what God prompts her to do, she believes God will give her the grace to do it. She states that she has spent so much of her life being lazy with loving by talking to people who are easy to love. She believes it will take a miracle to make her calm and loving enough to get her through to more difficult people. However, she is counting on miracles.

Mary Hart believes the Beloved Community is a good idea and a great goal. However, she thinks it is a thought for the far future. She believes that the American Dream has come a long way in developing, but there is still a lot of room for perfection. Mary believes that we are not as prejudiced against African Americans as we once were, but we are still denying others their rights as Americans. Like the Beloved Community, she believes the American Dream, will not happen soon. First, she believes we will have to gain the cooperation of everyone, and that will be an almost impossible task. Therefore, she believes humanity and our society have a long way to go before we can achieve and enjoy the benefits of the Beloved Community.

Mary expected the issues of social injustice to go beyond our history and our country in the Study Circle. However, she understands that we must learn from our past and it is important to revisit those issues before they come full circle, but there are many prevalent cases of social injustice in today's world that deserve immediate attention like the women in Iraq, the genocide in certain African countries, universal health care, child sweat shops, euthanasia, abortion, and the list goes on practically forever.

Mary believes racism and social injustice need to be taken more seriously in America. She states that the people in positions of power need to believe in the cause for social justice, because a law punishing social injustice would work. She believes that the public would be motivated by outside forces to act in a manner more socially acceptable and just. She thinks punishment or negative feedback for acts or words of social injustice would have to be started early in life, and the school systems would have to actively participate in it, and it would have to continue to be enforced throughout schooling and into the workplace. She thinks that a program or a mandatory program for adults would immediately address the issue, and then employers would have to enforce and oversee the results of the project. She thinks this concerted effort could work, especially if a program was started with young children.

Mary believes nonviolence is definitely the best approach considering the morals and ethics of today's society. She believes that violent methods contradict social justice in that the right to life is being denied. Mary believes that the media and voices of the world will be our key to achieving true social justice. Mary found that it was extremely disappointing when she read about the courts delivering the incorrect and unjust verdicts based on the apathy or perhaps antipathy towards the true meaning of the Constitution. She believes equality and sameness are very difficult issues to deal with in America, because equality and sameness are not always fair. She thinks there needs to be another aspect added in there, perhaps the aspect of merit or achievement through hard work.

Finally, in order to create a Beloved Community, Mary believes people must think of each other as equal and act out in love. For that to happen, she believes everyone must change. She understands that it is very difficult for people to change, especially those who are set in their ways. However, Mary believes that the creation of the Beloved Community can begin with one person living by the right standards and influencing and encouraging others to act and live in the same ways. She believes if one person influences only one more individual; the Beloved Community will be a success. However, she recognizes that the Beloved Community would be most successful in reaching out and touching others as a group.

Mary thinks she can act as an agent of change by treating people with justice, respect, and love. She believes that by showing others she cares for them will change the way they look at the world as well. She states she can stand up against acts of social injustice. She believes that she can confront those who infringe on the rights of others respectfully and in an appropriate manner. She also says that she can love people as well as verbally express her concern for society. She believes she can now join or form a larger group to make a bigger difference and to impact more people. She can now reach out and voice her concerns instead of keeping them to herself.

In conclusion, Mary believes as she reflects on her past experience with harassment, it would have been very difficult to reach out with love to someone who harassed you. She thinks she dealt with it the best she could at the time. She did not lash out at her harasser after the physical and verbal event. She managed to restrain her anger whenever she saw him. She brought the situation to those in a higher position. In her opinion, they took too long to carry out the verdict. In response, she persistently contacted those in higher power. Eventually her persistence paid off, and the situation was dealt with, not adequately, but it was dealt with. From that aspect, she can now relate to the Supreme Court's verdicts contradicting the Constitution case after case until they got it right. Based on the discussions and readings, she should have persisted until justice was served. She should have persisted until the verdict was just. She thought she should have known that more persistence would have brought a more just verdict. She states that she knows now that she can and will persist until justice is brought. She feels like she cannot give up fighting now.

The next and final chapter will provide the conclusion to the action research project by providing a summary of the citizens' knowledge level of the Beloved Community philosophy, Civil Rights cases, Nonviolent Resistance methodology, and Study Circle model as a result of participating in the Appalachian Study Circle for Social Justice. Then the final section of the final chapter will summarize the overall evaluations of the research project by the participants, professional peers, and researcher.

Chapter Five

REFLECTION, SUMMARY, AND CONCLUSION

Introduction

On Monday, May 2, 2005, the participants, known as the citizens of the Beloved Community Study Circle began to submit their exit surveys. The citizens of the Beloved Community Study Circle stated that the "Appalachian Study Circle for Social Justice: Creating a Beloved Community" was a good program and should be continued and developed. The citizens' knowledge of the study circle methodology increased as a result of completing the program. The citizens' knowledge of the nonviolence resistance method increased as a result of completing the module on Nonviolent Resistance. The citizens' knowledge of the Beloved Community increased as a result of completing the module on the Beloved Community. The citizens' knowledge of the landmark Civil Rights cases also increased as a result of completing the module on landmark Civil Rights cases. The citizens' understanding of their attitudes and beliefs on social justice increased after completing the four modules. The citizens gave the "Appalachian Study Circle for Social Justice: Creating a Beloved Community" an overall program rating of good to very good. The citizens completed the program with increased awareness of social injustice issues and additional skills to become a change agent in their community. The next section will discuss in more detail the citizens' knowledge levels of the study circle methodology.

Citizens Knowledge of Study Circle

The citizens' knowledge of the guided study circle methodology increased as a result of completing the study circle modules. Twenty percent of the citizens now rate their knowledge of the methodology of the study circle as above average. Tameka Jones started the study circle with an average knowledge of the methodology of study circles and completed the study circle with an above average knowledge of the study circle methodology. Eighty percent of the citizens now rate their knowledge of the methodology of study circles as average. Jill Scott started the study circle with an average knowledge of the methodology of the study circles and finished the study circle with an average knowledge of the study circle methodology. Fernando Torres started the study circle without any knowledge of the methodology of study circles and finished the study circle with an average knowledge of the study circle methodology. Karen Smith began the study circle without any knowledge of the methodology of study circles as well and ended the study circle with an average knowledge of the study circle methodology. Mary Hart also started the study circle without any knowledge of the methodology of the study circle methodology and ended the study circle with an average knowledge of the study circle methodology. The next section will discuss the citizens' final knowledge level of the nonviolent resistance method as a result of completing the study circle.

Citizens Knowledge of Nonviolent Resistant

The citizens' knowledge of the nonviolence resistance method increased as a result of completing the module on Nonviolent Resistance. Forty percent of the citizens' knowledge of the nonviolent resistance method did not increase and they rate their final knowledge of the nonviolent resistance method as average. Jill Scott began the study circle with an average knowledge of the nonviolent resistance method and completed the study circle with an average knowledge of the method. Karen Smith began the study circle with an average knowledge of the nonviolent resistance method and completed the study circle with an average knowledge. However, sixty percent of the citizens now rate their knowledge of the nonviolent resistance method as above average. Tameka Jones began the study circle with an average knowledge of the nonviolent resistance method and completed the study circle with an above average knowledge. Fernando Torres began the study circle without any knowledge of the nonviolent resistance method and completed the study circle with an above average knowledge of the method. Mary Hart began the study circle with an average knowledge of the nonviolent resistance method and completed the study circle with above average knowledge. The next section will discuss the citizens' knowledge level of the Beloved Community.

Citizens Knowledge of Beloved Community

The citizens' knowledge of the Beloved Community methodology increased as a result of completing the module on the Beloved Community. Forty percent of the citizens now rate their knowledge of the Beloved Community as average. Fernando Torres began the study circle without any knowledge of the Beloved Community and completed the study circle with an average knowledge. Karen Smith began the study circle without any knowledge of the Beloved Community and completed the study circle with an average knowledge of the Beloved Community. Forty percent of the citizens now rate their knowledge of the Beloved Community as above average. Tameka Jones began the study circle with a below average knowledge of the Beloved Community and completed the study circle with an above average knowledge. Mary Hart began the study circle with an average knowledge of the Beloved Community and finished the study circle with an above average knowledge. Twenty percent of the citizens rate their knowledge of the Beloved Community as below average. Jill Scott began the study circle with a below average knowledge of the Beloved Community and finished the study circle with a below average knowledge of the Beloved Community. The next section will discuss the citizens' knowledge of landmark Civil Rights cases.

Citizens Knowledge of Landmark Civil Rights Cases

The citizens' knowledge of the landmark Civil Rights cases increased as a result of the module on landmark cases. Eighty percent of the citizens started the study circle with a below average knowledge of landmark Civil Rights cases. Twenty percent of citizens started the study circle with an average knowledge of the landmark cases on Civil Rights. Forty percent of the citizens now rate their knowledge of the landmark Civil Rights cases as average. Fernando Torres began the study circle with a below average knowledge of the landmark Civil Rights cases and completed the study circle with an average knowledge of landmark cases. Karen Smith began the study circle with a below average knowledge of landmark Civil Rights cases and finished with an average knowledge of the landmark cases. Forty percent of the citizens now rate their knowledge of the landmark Civil Rights cases as above average. Tameka Jones began the study circle with a below average knowledge of landmark Civil Rights cases and ended with an above average knowledge of the landmark cases. Mary Hart began the study circle with an average knowledge of the landmark Civil Rights cases and ended with an above average knowledge of the landmark cases. Twenty percent of the citizens rate their knowledge of the landmark Civil Rights cases as below average. Jill Scott began the study circle with a below average knowledge of the landmark Civil Rights cases and ended the study circle with a below average knowledge of the landmark cases. The next section will discuss the citizens' overall evaluation of the study circle program.

Citizens Overall Program Evaluation

The citizens gave the "Appalachian Study Circle for Social Justice: Creating a Beloved Community" an overall rating of good to very good. Sixty percent of the citizens rate the overall program as good. Citizens Fernando Torres, Karen Smith, and Mary Hart rated the program as good. Forty percent of the citizens rate the overall program as very good. Citizens Jill Scott and Tameka Jones rated the program as very good.

Sixty percent of the citizens strongly agreed that the study circle questions were meaningful. Citizens Jill Scott, Tameka Jones, and Fernando Torres strongly agreed that the questions were important. Forty percent of the citizens agreed that the study circle questions were meaningful. Citizens Karen Smith and Mary Hart agreed that the questions were important.

Eighty percent of the citizens stated that the quantity of questions in each module was just right. Citizens Tameka Jones, Fernando Torres, Karen Smith, and Mary Hart thought the number of questions in each module was just right. Twenty percent of the citizens thought the quantity of questions in each session were too long. Citizen Jill Scott thought the number of questions in the modules were too long.

Sixty percent of the citizens thought the quantity of modules in the online program were just right. Citizens Fernando Torres, Karen Smith, and Mary Hart thought the number of the online sessions was just right. Forty percent of the citizens thought the quantity of modules were too short. Citizens Jill Scott and Tameka Jones thought the number of online sessions were too short.

Overall, the citizens thought the online program was a good program. The next section will discuss the citizens' attitudes and beliefs as a result of participating in the program.

Citizens Attitudes and Beliefs

The citizens' understanding of their attitudes and beliefs increased after completing the four modules. The citizens' understanding of others' attitudes and beliefs also increased as a result of participating in the study circle. Eighty percent of the citizens stated that their understanding of their attitudes and beliefs increased. Twenty percent of the citizens stated that they did not have any change in their attitudes and beliefs. Sixty percent of the citizens stated that their understanding of others' attitudes and beliefs increased. Forty percent of the citizens stated that they did not have any change in their understanding of others' attitudes and beliefs. The next section will discuss what the citizens liked most about the program.

Citizens Liked Most About Program

What did the citizens of the Beloved Community like most about the Beloved Community Study Circle? The citizens liked the information presented in each of the modules over the four-week online program. The citizens also liked the opportunity to face some hard questions and really understand and solidify many of their beliefs. The citizens found the program very interesting and stated that it covered a variety of topics that really helped them think differently. In conclusion, the citizens liked the idea of actually forming a Beloved Community, and would really like to see the idea of the Beloved Community go further. The next section will discuss what the citizens liked least about the program.

Citizens Liked Least About Program

What did the citizens of the Beloved Community like least about the study circle? The citizens felt there were so many levels of questions and journal entries that they thought too much was required in too short of a time period. The citizens felt they would have benefited from more time reading and responding to the modules. One citizen did not like the fact that the program curriculum consisted entirely of issues of the United States' past and no other countries. The citizens also stated it was hard to see where all the other citizens were coming from, because they did not respond to all the comments and questions in the "Join the Discussion" section. The citizens felt they would have learned even more if they had been able to read more of the other citizens' reactions and reflections as they went from module to module. Finally, one citizen felt he would have liked to meet the other citizens in person. The next section will provide the final comments from the citizens in the Beloved Community Study Circle.

Citizens Final Comments

The citizens thought the "Appalachia Study Circle for Social Justice: Creating a Beloved Community" was a good program and should continue and go further. The citizens were thankful for the opportunity to participate. One citizen wished her personal schedule had allowed for more involvement throughout the four modules. However, she felt her knowledge level and awareness level increased during the online sessions. The next and section will provide a professional association review of the program concept.

Professional Association Review

On Friday, July 15, 2005, the researcher submitted "The Beloved Community Guided Study Circle for Social Justice: Creating a Beloved Community" to the National Association of Student Personnel Administrators (NASPA) as a program proposal for the NASPA Student Affairs Multicultural Institute: Multiculturalism in the Context of Institutional Change and Strategic Priorities. On Tuesday, August 9, 2005, the director of educational programs provided the researcher with a copy of the reviewer comments of the Beloved Community Program. Upon review of the comments, the researcher thought that incorporating a summary of their evaluation would be an appropriate conclusion to the evaluation of the study circle.

The NASPA reviewers stated that the program exemplifies strategic partnerships, cultural competencies, and intercultural and interpersonal communication. The online part is most interesting and should help many dealing with issues to move beyond just the face-to-face conversations. The reviewers also stated the program looks very interesting, unique, and engaging. The program appears to be grounded in research and seems to be built upon the teachings of Dr. Martin Luther King, Jr. The content seemed very good and the expectations were clear.

The Program also demonstrates creativity and forward thinking. The reviewers also stated the proposal was fine but it could have been more specific regarding objectives, and the outcomes should be clarified. The next and final section of this book, *Appalachian Social Justice: Creating a Beloved Community,* will provide the conclusion with a summary of the goals, objectives and outcomes of the pilot program, the Appalachian Study Circle for Social Justice: Creating a Beloved Community.

Conclusion

In America, historically disenfranchised communities have a heritage of isolation and voicelessness as a result of the human condition: the sins of classism, racism and sexism. As an African American community leader, the researcher's passion has grown out of this heritage into a civic responsibility of empowering historically disadvantaged people to the extent that they are able to come out of economic, emotional, social and spiritual isolation and voicelessness. This action research project, the Beloved Community Study Circle for Social Justice, provided an unprecedented opportunity for the researcher, an Appalachian community leader, to utilize her passion for community empowerment to develop and implement a model for addressing social injustice in Appalachian communities.

The Beloved Community Study Circle asked the community of Morgantown, West Virginia to face a critical issue-how to build a Beloved Community. The study circle asked the community of Morgantown to get involved in an online community discussion by examining Dr. Martin Luther King, Jr.'s teachings on the Beloved Community and the nonviolent resistance method as tools to address issues of social injustices in our Appalachian community. There was an opportunity for people from all backgrounds and all parts of the community to participate in this constructive online conversation, and propose ways to build a Beloved Community as an individual change agent.

The Beloved Community Study Circle progressed over four consecutive weeks starting with a session on personal experience ("How does social injustice affect me?") to sessions providing broader perspectives ("What are others saying about social injustice?") to a session on action ("What can I do about the social injustice in my community?").

The citizens of the Beloved Community Study Circle stated that the "Appalachian Study Circle for Social Justice: Creating a Beloved Community" was a good program and should continue. The citizens' knowledge of the guided study circle methodology increased as a result of the study circle. The citizens' knowledge of nonviolence resistance increased as a result of the module on Nonviolent Resistance. The citizens' knowledge of the Beloved Community methodology also increased as a result of completing the module on the Beloved Community. The citizens' knowledge of the landmark Civil Rights cases increased as a result of the module on landmark cases. The citizens' understanding of their attitudes and beliefs increased after completing the four modules, and their understanding of others' attitudes and beliefs also increased as a result of participating in the study circle.

In addition to the increased knowledge as a result of participating in the study circle, the citizens felt there were so many levels of questions and journal entries that they thought too much was required in too short of a time period. The citizens felt they would have benefited from more time reading and responding to the modules. However, the citizens gave the "Appalachian Study Circle for Social Justice: Creating a Beloved Community" an overall rating of good to very good.

In conclusion, the participants of the Beloved Community Study Circle for Social Justice educated themselves on the issue of social justices, established new relationships, recognized ways to change their own behaviors, and learned how to become an individual change agent in their community.

Based on the feedback of the West Virginia peers, professional associates and the study circle participants, the researcher plans to duplicate the online project, the Appalachian Study Circle for Social Justice: Creating a Beloved Community, with the changes suggested by the participants. The first major change is to increase the number of modules to give participants more time to reflect and respond. The increased number of modules will also decrease the quantity of questions for each module and address the feedback about the high number of questions and journal entries required each week.

The second major change will be the creation of an electronic newsletter sent to each participant weekly to provide a summary of the reactions and reflections of each participant in response to the feedback of wanting to hear more from each participant throughout the study circle. The third major change will be the incorporation of a session to give the participants an opportunity to meet and talk to each other face to face. In conclusion, the Beloved Community Study Circles will be implemented in other Appalachian communities as a tool to discuss and address social injustices, isolation and voicelessness, with the support and sponsorship of other faith-based institutions committed to social justice.

The action research project, the Appalachian Study Circle for Social Justice: Creating a Beloved Community, is submitted as the first documented attempt to respond theologically to the legacy of isolation and voicelessness in this Appalachian community, Morgantown, West Virginia with a community development project, the Beloved Community Study Circle, developed from successful historical approaches to addressing social injustice. This theological response calls for a theology of liberation. This call required the making of an Appalachian liberation theology. The researcher has coined this theology as the "Appalachian Liberation Theology." The praxis of the Appalachian Liberation Theology is the Beloved Community Study Circle.

The study circle, a social analysis tool, has begun the systematic documentation of social injustices experienced by the people of Appalachian. This documentation is the first requirement of Appalachian Liberation Theology, because liberation theology requires the identification of the disenfranchised. Once the disenfranchised and their experiences with social injustice have been identified and documented, the experiences with social injustice are placed in the light of the Beloved Community and nonviolence resistance method, because the goal of the method of nonviolence resistance is the creation of the Beloved Community.

According to Dr. Martin Luther King, at the center of the nonviolence resistance method is the principle of love and this love is not sentimental or affectionate emotion, but this love is understanding and redeeming good will for all people. King believed we are able to love the person who does the evil deed while hating the deed in the creation of the Beloved Community. This method will also bring the full realization of the American Dream, a place of social justice. According to King, the American Dream is a place of respect for the dignity and worth of human personality. The Beloved Community calls for the recognition of the sacredness of human personality. In conclusion, the fourth week of the study circle challenged the participants to think as citizens of the Beloved Community.

The fourth week of the online community began with the question, "What individual actions can you take today in your community as a change agent to address social injustice?" Citizen Tameka Jones, after completing the Beloved Community Study Circle, thinks one step that she can take today in order to move toward a Beloved Community is to learn about the laws concerning social injustices. Another individual action she stated that she could take is to lead a forum concerning social injustices to get an idea how the community feels and maybe get insight into the reasons why people hate.

Tameka also thinks back on the social injustices that she experienced in the past, some of the situations she would have addressed the same, and other ones she would have done something differently. She thinks she would have questioned some people who made statements like "You talk like you are white," or people that called her a "nigger." As a result of participating in the study circle, Tameka has reclaimed her voice to respond to injustice in her response to the week four questions.

Citizen Fernando Torres states that the first thing that comes to mind in response to question four is obviously to take action. If he sees or finds out about any social injustice that is being committed against any of his friends, he will raise his voice and express his disapproval. As Fernando thinks about his past experience of being discriminated against in a fast food restaurant when he was not served and simply walked away, Fernando states he was really angry inside and still to this day he does not go to that place. However, given what he learned in the Beloved Community Study Circle, he thinks he acted in the right way, and he does not think he could act differently. However, he states that if he had the chance to go back to that situation, he would have written a letter to the local paper and or filed a complaint with the manager, but he still believes his initial actions represented nonviolence resistance. Citizen Fernando is also reclaiming his voice to speak out against injustice.

Citizen Karen Smith states that she can make herself remain compassionate towards individuals who commit injustice as a result of participating in the Beloved Community Study Circle. She states that she can now call an injustice an injustice when she sees it. She can raise her children to hate the sin while loving the sinner. She can educate others in her immediate sphere of influence about the injustices she sees. Karen states that she can see with all of this reflection under her belt that while she did not react aggressively to her son's teacher on the outside, her internal reaction was one of anger and extreme judgment.

While her awareness made her able to move around the injustice, she really did nothing to heal it. Now when she encounters such a situation in the future, she states she will be conscious enough of her internal reaction to pray out the anger and judgment. Then she will pray for healing, clarity, love, and grace for the individual who commits the injustice. If she feels prompted and capable, she will try to discuss the situation with the offender. Karen still has work on reclaiming her voice, but she has begun the first phase of reclaiming her voice. The first phase is becoming aware of your voicelessness.

Citizen Mary Hart believes that leading by actions is the most important step of all. If a person is seen supporting what they verbally say, more people are apt to follow them. Mary believes as she reflects on her past experience with harassment, it would have been very difficult to reach out with love to someone who harassed you. She thinks she dealt with it the best she could at the time. She brought the situation to the attention of someone in a higher position. In her opinion, they took too long to carry out the verdict. In response, she persistently contacted the authorities. Eventually her persistence paid off, and the situation was dealt with, not adequately, but it was dealt with.

Based on the discussions and readings, Mary now believes she should have persevered until justice was served. She should have fought until the verdict was just. She thought she should have known that more persistence would have brought a more just verdict. She states that she knows now that she can and will persist until justice is gained. Mary is coming out of personal isolation and is reclaiming her voice.

In conclusion, God is involved in the history of social justice in Appalachia. According to Appalachian theological reflection, the message of liberation articulated by the study circle methodology is a tool that is revealing the God of history because God is involved in the eradication of social injustice in Appalachia in order that the disenfranchised can reclaim their human dignity and create the Beloved Community.

Appalachian liberation theology is developing out of the need of Appalachian communities to think theological about their isolation and voicelessness and how to respond to the legacy of social injustice. The birthing of the Appalachian liberation theology represents the first self-conscious attempt by an Appalachian community leader and researcher to define the theology of Appalachian experience in the context of a history of isolation and voicelessness. The citizens of the Beloved Community are coming out of isolation and discovering their voices to speak against injustice. This book, *Appalachian Social Justice: Creating a Beloved Community*, chronicles the making of the Appalachian Liberation Theology.

BIBLIOGRAPHY

Adams, John Hurst and others, eds. *The Doctrine and Discipline of the African Methodist Episcopal Church.* Nashville, TN: The AMEC Sunday School Union, 1997.

Boff, Clodovis and Leonardo Boff. *Introducing Liberation Theology.* New York, NY: Orbis Books, 1988.

Brown v. Board of Education, 347 U.S. 483 (1954).

Church, F. Forrester. *The Essential Tillich.* New York. NY: Collier Books, 1987.

Cliff, Michele. "I Found God in Myself and I Loved Her/I Loved Her Fiercely," *Journal Of Feminist Studies in Religion (Spring 1986*): 7-39.

Cone, James H. *A Black Theology of Liberation.* New York, NY: Orbis Books, 1990.

________. *For My People.* New York, NY: Orbis Books, 1994.

________. *God of the Oppressed.* New York, NY: Harper San Francisco, 1975.

Cone, James H. and Gayraud S. Wilmore. *Black Theology: A Documentary History. Volume I: 1966-1979.* New York: Orbis Books, 1993.

________. *Black Theology: A Documentary History, Volume II: 1980-1992.* New York, NY: Orbis Books, 1993.

Evans, Mari-Lynn and others, eds. *The Appalachians: America's First and Last Frontier.* New York, NY: Random House, 2004.

Flavin-McDonald , Catherine and Martha L. McCoy. *Facing the Challenges of Racism and Race Relations*. Promfret, CT: Topfields Foundation, Inc., 1997.

Gandi, M.K. *Nonviolent Resistance (Satyagraha)*. New York, NY: Dover Publications, Inc., 2001.

Gordon, Mary R. "Historical Sketch of the Y.W.C.A." Typewritten: Wheeling, WV: West Virginia YWCA, 1916.

Gutierrez, Gustavo. *A Theology of Liberation*. New York, NY: Orbis Books, 2003.

Hood, Robert. *Must God Remain Greek?* Minneapolis, MN: Fortress Press, 1990.

International Bible Society. *The Holy Bible*. Grand Rapids, MI: International Bible Society Press, 1984.

King, Deborah H. "Multiple Jeopardy, Multiple Consciousness: The Context of a Black Feminist Ideology." *Signs* 14 (Autumn 1988): 42-72.

King, Martin L. *Strength to Love*. Philadelphia, PA: Fortress Press, 1963.

________. *The Measure of a Man*. Minneapolis, MN: Fortress Press, 2001.

Lincoln, C. Eric. *The Black Experience in Religion*. New York, NY: Anchor Books, 1974.

Marsh, Charles. *The Beloved Community: How Faith Shapes Social Justice from the Civil Rights Movement to Today*. New York, NY: Basic Books, 2005.

Miranda v. Arizona, 384 U.S. 436 (1966).

Neville, Robert Cummings. *A Theology Primer.* New York, NY: State University of New York Press, 1991.

The Paul J. Aicher Foundation. "Study Circle Resource Center," available from http://www.studycircles.org/en/Page/WhoWeAre.aspx; Internet; accessed 10 July 2005.

Plessy v. Ferguson, 163 U.S. 537 (1896).

Rivera-Watson, Carmen, ed. "Racial Justice Training Manual." New York, NY: YWCA of the USA, 1996.

Ruether, Rosemary Radford. *Sexism and God-Talk.* Boston, MA: Beacon Press, 1983.

Russell, Valerie, "Collective Struggle: A Minority Woman's Point of View on Racism/Sexism." *Concern Magazine* (January 1982): 30-32.

Sample, Tex. *The Spectacle of Worship in a Wired World.* Nashville, TN: Abingdon Press, 1998.

Salving. Valerie, "The Human Situation: A Feminine View." *The Journal of Religion.* (April 1960): 25-41.

Scott v. Sanford, 60 U.S. 393 (1857).

Street Law and Supreme Court Historical Society. "Landmark Supreme Court Cases," available from http://landmarkcases.org/plessy/equal_same.html; Internet; accessed 25 March 2005.

Walker, Alice. *The Color Purple*. New York, NY: Harcourt Brace Jovanovich, 1982.

Washington, James M. *A Testament of Hope.* New York, NY: Harper San Francisco, 1986.

West, Cornel. *Race Matters.* New York, NY: Vintage Books, 2001.

Index*

---

* This index was created with **TExtract™**